HeartPath PRACTITIONER:

A Practitioner's Guide

Cinthia McFeature, Ph.D.
& Bill McFeature, Ph.D.

HeartPath PRACTITIONER:
A Practitioner's Guide
The Healing Journey through the Life Narrative into the Heart of the Divine

Tate Publishing & *Enterprises*

Published by Tate Publishing & Enterprises, LLC
127 E. Trade Center Terrace | Mustang, Oklahoma 73064 USA
1.888.361.9473 | www.tatepublishing.com

Tate Publishing is committed to excellence in the publishing industry. The company reflects the philosophy established by the founders, based on Psalm 68:11,
"The Lord gave the word and great was the company of those who published it."

Cover design by Kellie Southerland
Interior design by Nathan Harmony
Chapter logo design by Deanna Grant

Published in the United States of America

ISBN: 978-1-60799-811-2
1. Psychology: Psychopathology: General
2. Religion: Christian Ministry: Counseling & Recovery
09.07.23

Dedication

This book is dedicated to all who seek the Heart of God and the path of compassion by offering healing through the Spirit, which is transformational and life changing into eternity.

Table of Contents

Authors' Note to Practitioners

This book is useful for practitioners working with a diverse clientele who possess a variety of behavioral and emotional problems. The psycho-spiritual principles and processes of the *HeartPath Practitioner* can assist anyone who works in the healing arts to bring to awareness a healing journey for each and every client. The healing process begins with the "told story" and making sense of an individual's reported lived experience.

HeartPath principles are grounded in phenomenological inquiry and narrative approaches that allow the healing journey to exist between the practitioner and the client. HeartPath is considered a transformative practice to create and transcend to various forms of consciousness and mindfulness living. We offer this book as a guide for all practitioners to co-create with his or her clients a testimony reflective of the client's healing journey. At all times, the *HeartPath Practitioner* honors the divine in others and within themselves.

Brain research has shown the impact that stress can have on our heart. The heart, metaphorically, is symbolic to a "portal to the soul." The *HeartPath Practitioner* simply makes a connection between illness and networks of pathology. The concept of HeartPath was developed, formulated, and is grounded in sound brain, cardiovascular, and narrative research. The focus of HeartPath interventions speaks to an individual's healing journey as a whole being—physical, emotional, mental, and spiritual. True healing takes place in an integrative, holistic approach to a multidimensional being that addresses all areas. If any part of the human being—emotional, physical, mental, or spiritual—is not in harmony, it will affect another area of our well-being. This process perpetuates a cycle of illness due to underlying issues not being addressed.

Introduction

> A HeartPath practitioner is best defined as a practitioner who offers counsel to his or her clients from a heart of compassion. This includes being fully present to the heart of God within the sacred space of the heart connection and a higher God consciousness. The HeartPath practitioner will see through a spiritual prism of compassion in order to help his or her clients connect to their own HeartPath, which is guided by the love and spiritual light within our being. The power of the told story/narrative approach reflects the healing journey. The HeartPath philosophy speaks to the balance of emotional, mental, spiritual, and physical self. It is a matter of the heart, and it is here that the true transformation for healing occurs.

The Creator has a reason for everything and a rhythm to everything that he has created. The first organ formed in a mother's womb is the heart. The heartbeat is the beginning of the firing of neurons in the brain, which then take over to monitor the heartbeat. The heart is equipped with an electromagnetic field that extends beyond the body between five to eight feet. The inner sanctuary of the heart is the seat of the spirit that connects with the spirit of the divine.

The HeartPath philosophy speaks to the balance of life through physical, mental, emotional, and spiritual health. The four basic assessment principles of HeartPath are as follows:

- Presenting strong emotional issues can have an effect on the physical body. Discover and heal the core emotional issue and you may address and heal the physical ailment.
- A mental block can be traced back to an emotional issue. Free the mental block and you may address and heal the emotional issue.
- Intuitive (psychological) error causes mental blocks. Release and heal the intuitive error and the mental block is dissolved.
- With a spiritual disconnection there is always confusion and intuitive error. Reconnect through faith and heal the spiritual disconnection by connecting with the spirit of the divine source and there can be no intuitive error.

Our heart is constantly connecting with other hearts through spiritual intuitiveness, rhythm of the universe, and all creation. Gordon MacDonald stated, "The heart, probably the strongest and most resilient of our muscles, is designed to be still between every beat. Most growing things observe a period of dormancy every year. Every cycle is completed by a period of stillness." The rhythm of the universe connects to the heartbeat of the earth and the heartbeat of all creation.

Research has shown that the *narrative*, or "thoughts in text," connects to an emotion forming a feeling that manifests in the human heart. A seven-year-old made the following statement: "When we are angry, our hearts shrink and then become flat." Interestingly, research has recently revealed that when a thought induces an emotion such as anger, the feeling process occurs and our DNA shrinks, but when a thought induces a feeling such as elation, then feelings such as love and compassion occur, and our DNA relaxes and spreads out. When DNA is in a relaxed state, it improves our immune system (Braden, 2008). Research has shown that when a person is under emotional distress, physical illness will many times follow. The weakening of our immune system makes us vulnerable to physical illness.

There is a power in our thoughts that generates dialogue or conversational content. We create our own surroundings by the thoughts we think, which in turn develop an individual's "telling of the story."

There are also external and internal factors that affect the heart, such as traumatic events, relationships, physical challenges, mental challenges, seasons of change, world events, media, emotional challenges, and spiritual challenges. These memories are created through the lived experiences that can have a significant impact on our life journeys. Research shows us that the heart has a profound memory function that connects with our four life domains or dimensions of our "whole being"—physical, mental, emotional, and spiritual.

The HeartPath journey requires the principles of reflection, illumination of the human soul, a sense of compassion, intention, and knowing oneself through the use of the narrative process that depicts an individual's "telling of the story." The HeartPath journey follows the heart by awakening the spirit of the inner heart and opening the gift of intuition.

> "Desperate days are the stepping-stones on the path of light."
>
> —Streams in the Desert

> "Of all earthly music that which reachest farthest into heaven is the beating of a truly loving heart."
>
> —Henry Ward Beecher

Chapter One
Physiology of the Heart

> *"Christ shall come to thee showing thee his consolation if thou make for him within thee a worthy dwelling place; all his glory and honour is within and there is his plesaunce."*
>
> —Thomas à Kempis, 1379–1471

There is a peace deep within the inner heart that brings health to your body, to your mind, and to your heart. The physiology of the heart in its own essence reveals to us so much more about the power within to heal. The lifeblood that our hearts pump carries our unique and individual DNA that connects us to the heart of our Creator. This chapter will go over various aspects of the physiology of the heart and begins our journey toward understanding healing.

Integrative behavioral health approaches are rapidly developing in today's time. The pioneering efforts of behavioral integrative approaches are well grounded in empirical research as it pertains to our "physical heart." The dilemma that faces the primary care practitioner and the mental health practitioner is: "Where do we locate the causes of any illness?"

Biology of the Heart

The heart is the organ at the center of our being, connected to all that God created us to be in our physical bodies as it pumps our lifeblood, our emotions, our minds, and our spiritual self. Considering the physiological effects of a heart is important to begin to understand how this magnificent organ is more powerful than has been given credit. This chapter will help us to reflect on the great significance of the heart from a physiological perspective and how interconnected the heart is to our whole being.

The heart is a type of mechanical pump weighing approximately ten ounces; it beats an average of seventy-two times a minute and more than one hundred thousand times a day. Science reveals that the heart is the first organ created approximately twenty-two days from conception. The heart beats with a rhythm of perfect unison. It is the beat of the heart that provides an electrical impulse that activates the brain-functioning processes. The heartbeat will increase and peak at about 157 beats per minute prior to coming under control of the brain at about ten to twelve weeks. The heartbeat will then decrease over nine months.

The mind-heart connection can be explained from a physiological standpoint. Research in the area of neurocardiology demonstrated that with each beat of the heart, the heart sends complex signals to the brain and other organs. The heart also communicates with the brain and other organs through the production of hormones and neurotransmitters by producing a hormone called *atrial natriuretic factor (ANF)*. The heart, therefore, operates as a sensory organ, hormone-producing gland, and information-processing center.

The heart does much more than pump blood continuously throughout life. As our body changes, so does the demand for oxygen, and the heart responds to this need. The heart works differently during sleep than in the middle of a three-mile run. The heart and circulatory system can respond almost instantaneously to shifting situations. This includes instances such as when a person stands up or lies down or when a person is faced with a dangerous situation.

Electromagnetic Heart Functions

The heart is not like most muscles that rely on nerve impulses to cause them to contract. The heart muscle contracts on its own accord. The heart has muscle cells that have the ability to contract spontaneously, and these cells work by generating electrical signals that spread to the rest of the heart and cause it to contract with a regular, steady beat. This electrical signal is known as the *electromagnetic heart function*.

The heartbeat actually begins with a small group of specialized muscle cells located in the upper right-hand corner of the right atrium. This area of the heart is known as the sinoatorial (SA) node. The cells in the SA node generate their electrical signals more frequently than cells elsewhere in the heart in order for the electrical signals generated by the SA node to synchronize the electrical signals traveling to the rest of the heart. For this reason, the SA node is also known as the heart's pacemaker or rhythm-maker.

In 1903, William Einthoven, a Dutch physiologist and Nobel laureate, founded the modern field of electrocardiography. Einthoven invented the string galvanometer, making it possible to do precise measurements of the electrical activity produced by the beating human heart.

Einthoven was trained in medicine but had a profound interest in physics that led to many inventions of devices used to measure and record physiological activities in the human body. A key challenge for physiologists at that time was measuring the electrical activity associated with the beating heart. By the 1880s, it was known that each contraction of the heart produces electrical changes throughout the body, but physiologists were unable to find a method for making immediate, reliable measurements of this activity. One device used a column of mercury that rose and fell with changes in the electric current, but measurements required so much time and so many calculations that the device was useless for making practical observations.

Around 1903, Einthoven solved this problem when he invented his string galvanometer. The device consisted of a very thin wire of quartz held in a magnetic field. The instrument was extremely sensitive; the wire would move in reaction to even the smallest electric current. By magnifying the wire and recording its movements on film, Einthoven could make precise measurements of the heart's electrical activity.

Quantum physics considers the smallest discrete quantity of a physical property, for example, electromagnetic radiation or angular momentum, as a connection to everything in the universe and our heart's energy. This phenomenon should induce a curiosity about the HeartPath connection and how far it reaches, even into eternity.

Research conducted by the Institute of HeartMath has documented that there is a doughnut-shaped field of energy that surrounds the heart and extends beyond the body between five to eight feet. This is a field of electromagnetic energy that is a configuration called a "torus." This heart field is not to be confused with the body's aura, but based on what the aura reveals, this may be the center where the aura actually begins. The HeartPath practitioner can learn to tune into this field when working with their clients. Noting the personal space acceptability with different individuals and the energy that is projected and solidified from their personal fear and pain is one way the HeartPath practitioner can assess and be in touch heart to heart.

According to Paul Pearsall, Ph.D., a psychoneuroimmunologist, revealed in his book, *The Heart's Code*, new findings about cellular memories and the role they play in the mind/body/spirit connection. His research was based on heart transplant recipients who reported memories that were not his or her own, but belonged to the heart donor. The energy cardiology practitioners have introduced Cardiac Synchronized Energy Patterns, which is a way of detecting energy associated with the heart. These include electrical activity (recorded by electrocardiograph), magnetic activity (recorded by the magnetocardiograph), cardiac sounds (recorded by an electronic stethoscope), and various pressure and temperature changes (recorded by specially-designed quantifying instruments). Energy cardiology can then study synchronization between organisms that are not physically connected.

The World Health Organization defines the electromagnetic field as electric fields that are created by differences in voltage; the higher the voltage, the stronger will be the resultant field. Magnetic fields are created when electric current flows; the greater the current, the stronger the magnetic field. An electric field will exist even when there is no current flowing. If current does flow, the strength of the magnetic field will vary with power consumption, but the electric field strength will be constant. Looking at this from a universe perspective, if we observe an electric field, we should understand that a magnetic field is generated proportional to the strength of the current. Likewise, where we see a magnetic field, we should understand that it derives from the underlying motion of charged particles and that its strength derives from the strength of the underlying current. The implications are simple, yet far-reaching.

Magnetic fields have been strongly implicated in everything from star formation to black holes within the structure and the evolution of galaxies and galaxy clusters. If magnetic fields are held at least partially responsible for the structure and function of the universe, then, by extension, the electric currents are equally important in the structure and function of the universe. If the universe and galaxies are threaded by magnetic fields, then they are equally threaded by the electric currents from which the magnetic fields arise.

Psychocardiology

Psychocardiology is a new field emerging that goes back to the 1920s. Psychological problems, such as depression, anxiety, and social isolation seem to predict both the development of disease in healthy and medically complicated patients. Psychologists are exploring the role of external environmental factors such as the role of socioeconomic status. It appears that heart disease affects both the upper class with noted stressors as well as people who have low education, low income, and low-prestige jobs also with life stressors. The stressors of discrimination, bad jobs, and crime then heighten chronic stressors. This heightened physiological responsiveness and unhealthy behavior can lead to increased stress, leaving these individuals at greater risk of heart disease.

It is important for practitioners to learn more about heart disease and communicate ways to prevent heart disease with their patients. Practitioners in such fields as healing arts, psychology, counseling, neurology, and cardiology should work together as they look at the patient's need for both preventive and aftercare from heart surgery. HeartPath practitioners from all fields of medicine and behavioral health care can communicate to their clients through behavioral interventions helpful in addressing major heart disease risk factors, including smoking, physical inactivity, and diabetes. Smoking, for example, increases blood pressure, decreases exercise tolerance, increases the tendency for blood to clot, and decreases "good" cholesterol.

Dean Ornish, M.D., teaches that among the deeper causes of heart disease are psychosocial factors such as isolation, loneliness, and alienation. Dr. Ornish developed a lifestyle program called "*Opening Your Heart*," which is designed to educate patients, and the patient's families in coordination with their physicians, that the most effective way to open blocked arteries may be by opening one's heart emotionally and spiritually as well. Many medical professionals are now beginning to see the heart as a reflection of how we live our lives. The HeartPath practitioner keeps all of this in mind when providing counsel to the client. Lifestyle changes may involve changes in diet and stress management as an alternative to cardiac surgery and/or medications. Dr. Ornish concurs with other medical professionals that heart disease can be reversed without surgery or medications in many cases.

If we work at these deeper levels, clients are much more likely to choose and maintain lifestyles that are life enhancing rather than self-destructive. They may say, "Maybe I'll live longer," but that's not the point. Health is only a means to an end; it's not an end in itself.

Psychoneurocardiology

Bypass surgery may be seen as a metaphor for an incomplete approach to dealing with a life-threatening problem. Research has proven that the heart is more than just a pump and, therefore, is imported by emotions, psychosocial (relationships), and spiritual connections. It's a vision that attempts to integrate medical knowledge with a deeper, ancient wisdom. Dr. Ornish stated that in modern medical terminology, we could call our program a multifactorial intervention that includes diet, stress management, smoking cessation, exercise, and healthy social support, or, perhaps more simply, *psychoneurocardiology*.

Psychoneurocardiology is a new field that is a multifactorial intervention that includes diet, stress management, smoking cessation, exercise, and group support. Listed below are the basic principles of caring for your heart that should be your lifestyle as you follow the HeartPath:

1. Exercise: Regular exercise is one of the biggest factors in maintaining cardiovascular health. As you exercise, you can speak out loud or in your mind an affirmation of healing, such as "Healthy body, healthy mind, healthy spirit, and healthy heart." You can repeat this in rhythm with your workout with faith and pure intention.
2. Proper Diet: Try to avoid all fatty meats as the death-dealing foods they are. Look for flavorful ways to prepare salmon and other fish; the Internet has many recipes, and there are specific cookbooks that deal with heart-care diets.
3. Blood Pressure: Check it periodically and do what it takes to keep it in the healthy range. According to the National Institutes of Health, doctors are recommending that your blood pressure be below the 120 systolic blood pressure and below 80 diastolic blood pressure.
4. Cholesterol: Have your cholesterol checked for both HDL and LDL levels and work hard to keep them in

the normal range. According to the American Heart Association, your total blood cholesterol will fall into one of these categories: desirable: less than 200 mg/dL; borderline high risk: 200–239 mg/dL; high risk: 240 mg/dL and over. The good cholesterol is also important and should be over 40. Medium-chain fats of coconut oil, avocado, and olive oil provide fats our bodies need.

5. Smoking: Quit. Or never start. If it didn't matter, no one would say a word.
6. Weight: Excess weight taxes the heart way too much, so if you're serious about cardiovascular health, find a way to manage the extra pounds through diet and exercise monitored by your doctor.
7. Stress: In most universal teachings, including the Bible, the heart is considered the seat of our emotions. Remaining calm during times of stress rather than "flying off the handle" not only maintains peace with associates, but it helps keep the heart muscle strong and healthy for a lifetime. Conversely, rage and anger significantly weaken this primary organ.

Listed below are heart-healthy foods to add to your diet that have been proven to make a difference in our hearts' health. We recommend organic foods when available.

1. Apples: Plenty of pectin to help maintain healthy cholesterol levels, plus potassium for blood pressure

2. Beans: Lots of good fiber and folic acid for healthy levels of homocysteine

3. Garlic: Can help maintain cholesterol health and keeps blood flowing freely

4. Grapes: Contain powerful oligomeric proanthocyanidins (OPCs), which are also present in a wide variety of fruits and vegetables, along with resveratrol, which lend antioxidant support to heart cells and strengthen the vascular system

5. Nuts: Are full of magnesium and monounsaturated oils, which are the good kind of fats that promote cardiovascular health

6. Oatmeal: Keeps cholesterol in check with fiber and a polysaccharide called beta-glucan

7. Pomegranate Juice: This has more heart-healthy polyphenols than the equivalent amount of red wine or green tea. Helps keep arteries clean and cholesterol levels healthy

8. Salmon: Is the best source of critical omega-3 essential fatty acids

9. Soy (Organic Only): Isoflavones in soy can reduce cholesterol

10. Virgin coconut oil

Each session is an opportunity to discuss a lifestyle of movement and exercise to enforce overall daily living activity (DLA). Some form of exercise not only promotes a healthy heart, but also creates endorphins that reduce depression levels.

The HeartPath practitioner should spend time educating their client about ways they can keep their heart's healthy. This is always in coordination with the client's primary care practitioner. This process will vary by individual and should be addressed on a case-by-case basis. For example, a thirty-year-old male would be willing and able to do certain things to keep his heart healthy, whereas an eighty-year-old male would have a different health plan. The HeartPath practitioner takes into consideration the importance of having a strong and healthy heart and all that entails. Many individuals refer to the human body as the temple of the spirit of God. Proper nutrition, simple exercise, and regular checkups by your doctor have been proven to make us aware of keeping our hearts healthy.

In the United States, and many other industrialized countries, heart disease is the leading cause of death. According to the United States Centers for Disease Control and Prevention (CDC), more than 710,000 people in the United States die of heart disease each year. Every thirty-five seconds, an American dies of heart disease or stroke. Cardiovascular disease kills more Americans than any other medical condition. In addition, more than 70 million live with these conditions.

The HeartPath practitioner is aware of the things in life that have an effect on the heart from a physiological, emotional, mental, and spiritual position. These include, but are not limited to, traumatic life events, relationship issues, physical health challenges, combinations of financial, employment, and other life pressures, changes in the seasons, and world events experienced or as presented by the media. The effect may impact one or more of these areas: heart-physical impact, heart-mental impact, heart-emotional impact, and heart-spiritual impact.

The Deeper Causes of Heart Disease

> "The real epidemic in our culture is not just physical heart disease; it's what I call emotional and spiritual heart disease: The sense of loneliness, isolation, and alienation that is so prevalent in our culture."
>
> —Dean Ornish, 1993

In the late 1950s, research linked stress to an increased risk of cardiovascular disease. In addition, adverse psychological factors such as depression, chronic anger, social isolation, and certain kinds of anxiety have an overall effect on your health. What goes hand in hand with these psychological factors are other unhealthy lifestyle choices such as smoking, excessive drinking of alcohol, overeating, lack of exercise, and lack of sleep, all dealing with an attempt to cope with negative thoughts or mask them.

Excessive chronic overstimulation of the sympathetic nervous system, which causes "fight or flight," can be responsible for physiological changes that promote atherosclerosis, the slow buildup of plaque deposits in the arteries of the heart. It is important for the HeartPath practitioner to point out the signs of stress, which may include feeling irritable, difficulty sleeping, over- or undereating, difficulty concentrating, abusing alcohol or drugs, feeling anxious, gaining or losing excessive amounts of weight, and feeling overwhelmed at home or work.

This book will serve as an overview of what it takes to follow the HeartPath from the mind, emotions, and spirit, but also to help you focus on the importance of balance of the physical body. We need to consider the importance and significance of the heart in relationship to our physical well-being, the center of our being, which circulates lifeblood to all other organs in our body. Therefore, it is recommended that individuals considering the HeartPath are educated in caring for the heart from a physiological perspective. By doing so, maybe we can change the fact that the leading cause of death in the United States and other industrialized countries is heart disease.

Research has revealed that the heart communicates with the brain and the rest of the body in three ways: 1) neurologically (transmission of nerve impulses); 2) biochemically (through hormones and neurotransmitters); and 3) biophysically (through pressure waves). There is also growing scientific evidence that suggests the heart may also communicate with the brain and body in a fourth way—energetically (through electromagnetic field interactions), which was mentioned earlier in this chapter. The following chapter will attempt to bridge the HeartPath with the narrative integration of the "telling of the story." Our life stories are unique to our life path, but what we begin to see and understand is the HeartPath leads us to one place, the road home into the heart of God.

These identified biophysiological communication

pathways between the mind and body connection, discussed in chapter one, yield to the importance of the mind-narrative processes. This phenomenon allows the narrative construction of the "telling of the story."

Chapter Two
Brain-Mind-Narrative Integration

"With our thoughts we make the world."

—Buddha

Emerging Mind

The mind emerges from brain activity, which is shaped by interpersonal experiences. We synthesize concepts from information processing, memory, narrative, and neurobiology. Mental representations form *themes* or schema through which *implicit memory* allows the mind to create generalizations and summaries of past experiences. These representational themes are then used to present cognition for rapid analysis of ongoing perception. The formation of themes or patterns is the essential manner in which the brain learns from past experiences and then directly influences the present and shapes future actions. The heart-mind connection occurs when the actions (decisions an individual makes) are derived from our thoughts with the heart's intentions, which appear to activate the resulting actions. This includes an individual's spiritual belief system and the faith that reflects a spiritual foundation. An important determinant of the quality of a narrative is the cognitive mechanisms that provide the basic building blocks required for the "telling of a story."

Daniel Siegel, M.D., stated that current brain research findings stem from human development and neurobiology, which brings a whole new understanding of the mind. The human mind emerges from the flow of electrical impulses within the brain. The mind is created when neurophysiological processes and interpersonal experiences interact in the brain. Overall, human beings' interactions shape the function of neural impulses bringing forth the emerging mind.

The mind is unseen by the naked eye, but it is as real as the heart or brain. The mind reflects the connection between brain structure and function. The mind is about the activation of neural energy and the flow of information.

The mind has portholes of processing information. Our sensory systems that respond to stimuli from outside the body represent information that has manifested from these neural impulses and serve as mental symbols. The integration of these portholes of processing information into a coherent whole is a key focus of "making sense" of the derived information, the lived experiences. Siegel stated that interpersonal relationships might facilitate this drive to integrate a coherent experience. Relationships may shape the structures that create mental representations of lived experience and allow a coherent view of our world.

Interpersonal experiences directly influence how we

mentally construct reality. This shaping process occurs throughout life. Brain research suggests that emotion serves as a central organizing process within the brain. An individual's ability to organize emotions is a byproduct that directly shapes the ability of the mind to integrate lived experiences and to adapt to future stressors.

Memory Function

Memory forms will be discussed in this chapter to best help us understand how our lived experiences shape not only what we remember, but how we remember and, in turn, how we shape the narratives of our lives. Memory can be seen as the way the mind encodes elements of lived experience into forms of mental representations.

The way the mind attempts to integrate these mental representations is within the *narrative* process. *Autobiographical narratives* are reflected upon in order to make sense of an individual's lived experiences and provide some form of coherence to the emerging mind. In retrospect, the capacity of the mind to represent and process mental activity of both self and others is a concept that promotes the connectiveness within relational domains.

Memory function is defined as how lived experiences impact future function. The brain experiences the world and encodes this lived experience in a manner that alters the way we respond in the future. The emphasis is that lived experience shapes the structure of the brain. Siegel stated that this process is referred to as "experience-dependent" brain development. We should continue to understand that our brains and our minds mirror ongoing development across each individual's lifespan.

An individual can recall past events that are determined by the brain creating a mental representation or image of an event or experience within the mind. This is called encoding a memory. The next stage of this process is referred to as memory storage, which speaks to the change in probability of activating a particular neural network pattern in the future. Memory is a process that is based on altering probability of a neuronal firing system.

Our memories are based on the binding together of neuronal activated patterns. When multiple sensory systems of hearing, seeing, touch, and smell become associated, it is more likely that these experiences will be reactivated during the retrieval process. These mental representations are linked together by a wide range of internal mental processes unique to each individual.

These mental representations are embedded into the basic components of implicit memory. Our minds use mental representations of the world in order to assess a situation and to determine what the next future moment in time may bring to an individual. *Explicit memory* is retrieved episodically, which requires focal and conscious attention. This type of memory we can recall from factual information.

Autobiographical Memory

The distinct aspects of memory are thought to involve different centers of activation within the brain. For example, semantic recall appears to involve a dominance of left-over-right hippocampal activation. Autobiographical recall, in contrast, involves more of the right hippocampus and right orbitofrontal cortex. Here we can see that structure and function within the brain correlate with our day-to-day encounters with subjective experience.

Within explicit autobiographical memory, we find a reflection of self in time. This generic episodic recollection can be identified as a general description summating across your perception over a range of time regarding specific episodes. In a sense, this is self-concept or self-schema made conscious about your self.

Lived experiences that involve minimal emotional intensity seem to possess focal attention and have a higher likelihood of being registered as "unimportant" and, therefore, not easily recalled at a later date. However, lived experiences with a moderate to high degree of emotional intensity seem to be defined as "important," probably by anatomic structures in the limbic system, such as the amygdala and orbitofrontal cortex, and are more easily remembered in the future.

The authors focus on the importance of understanding the degree of stress and its direct effect on memory. The effects of stress appear to be mediated by the neuroendocrine responses, which produce an immediate effect of noradrenalin release and the more sustained effects of glucocorticoids, such as cortisol or stress hormones.

Memory forms the foundation for both the implicit reality, such as behavioral responses, emotional reactions, perceptual-motor, and schemata of self and others in the world. Explicit memory recollects factual information of the self across our lifespan. We must understand the conscious and subconscious layers of memory in order to comprehend other individuals' present and past lived experiences.

Memory and Narrative Connection

This next section will attempt to make a connection between memory and narrative (verbal and nonverbal), which will speak to the individual's "told story." The identification of client within the text of this book will be applied best to illustrate the impact and therapeutic value of narrative interventions utilized in the healing/counseling arts. This connection between our interpersonal interactions and self-process is truly seen as an important aspect of memory, the "telling of our lived experience."

The telling of a client's lived experience and/or life story plays a significant role in the client's healing journey. The narrative is stored memory and recall ability of the client's lived experience in a story format. Co-construction between the practitioner and the client's narrative is a fundamental process, reflecting parts of an individual's subconscious and conscious worlds. The origin of narrative is revealed through compassionate and personal mental processes involving self-reflection.

The life story narrative captures attention from both the practitioner and client, requiring participation by both parties to actively construct one's lived experience. This relates to the "presence" of the practitioner with compassion to listen with intention.

The lived experience or life story involves an individual's perspective, various characters and activities, mental states (emotions, beliefs, memories, and intentions), and identification of conflicts and resolutions.

Autobiographical Narrative

An *autobiographical narrative* will incorporate generalizations from lived experiences and aspects of imagined events or experiences. The emergence of a life story and/or lived experience may involve a stratum of narrative genres reflected in fiction, fact, and schemata (described events). Life stories come in the form of daily routines, myths, films, plays, novels, diary notes, conversations, or coaching or counseling sessions. Narrative is a fundamental process that has a revealing and therapeutic value in creating the shared story, the determinants of behavior patterns, and may influence our internal world, our dreams, imagery, sensations, and mental states of mind.

The "*telling of the story*" process involves both verbalization and nonverbal signs that are received by the practitioner and then communicated back to the client. This interpersonal interaction between the practitioner and client shares the existence of objective and lived subjective experiences of the client. This therapeutic relationship allows the creation of narrative coherence or "making sense" of the client's "told story." For example, guided imagery is a technique that may bring forth the client's lived experiences of life. Guided imagery is the use of a combination of relaxation and mental visualization to assist the client in the healing process. The practitioner guides the defining process of a client's narrative by identifying how lived experience is shaped by common and unique narrative themes present in his or her lives. Recognizing the significance of generated themes, reflecting "a make sense out of a client's told story," is a key factor when reflecting information back to the client. The unconscious mental representations may also be revealed as narrative themes. The coherence-creating narrative process has a unifying quality that links aspects of memory-creating behavioral manifestations that represent past, present, and future. The mental representations of implicit memory assist in organizing the themes of how the details of explicit autobiographical memory are expressed within a life story or lived experiences as told by the individual.

Our present state of mind reflects the social context in which our narrative is being told. We formulate together selected recollections and imagined details to create a story generated by past events, as well as by the practitioner engaging in listening to the told story. We must keep in mind that the very social nature of narrative defines the self and, therefore, is always in the process of creating itself within new lived experiences that eventually reflect the told story. The story unfolds in its own creation and lights our path to the heart of who we are and why we are here.

Chapter Three

Belief Systems Relative to the HeartPath

"You are in that place to testify."
—Emerson's Journal, 1803–1882

Universal Heart

The HeartPath practitioner takes into consideration the significance of the heart throughout the history of mankind relevant to the heart-mind-spirit connection. The HeartPath practitioner understands the connecting love of an invisible bridge between the whole being and the divine. Therefore, it is important to have an understanding of the different belief systems that have attempted to frame this healing connection.

The ancient Greeks believed that the heart was the seat of intelligence. Other spiritual literature refers to the heart as the heart chakra to denote the heart center, the *latifa* that is called "*akhfa*," which means "the most hidden." Others believed the heart to be the source of the soul or of the emotions. The idea that the heart is the source of emotions is an idea that persists in today's western culture.

Many of the ancients taught that the mind existed beyond the brain confined within the skull of the human body. Some taught that the mind was a field of energy and information that extended from the brain stem out beyond and about the head and the crown chakra. Some taught that the mind was centered closer to the heart chakra.

Thousands of years ago, ancient scientists in India described the energy systems that exist in our subtle bodies or energy fields. The Indian yogis called these centers wheels, or chakras in Sanskrit. These chakras or energy vortices are seen to spin like wheels.

In the past, western culture and medicine chose to consider this valuable information from Yogic and Ayurvedic literature and from the teachings and practice of acupuncture with its roots in China as primitive and unscientific. With modern technology, science can now measure these subtle energies at the chakras and the acupuncture meridians.

These chakras take in the higher frequency vibrations and transmute them into vibrations utilizable by the physical body. This lower frequency vibration transmutes or translates into hormonal activity within the physical body to cause physiological and then cellular changes. These ancient yogic teachings hold true with seven major chakras within the physical body. Each chakra is associated with a major endocrine gland and a major nerve plexus. The heart chakra is the fourth chakra and embraces emotion. The heart chakra holds the key to unconditional love, pure energy of the universe, which is the balance of energy, color, and light.

The Heart Sutra is usually considered a member of the Perfection of Wisdom, along with the Diamond Sutra, and is considered by many to be the primary representative of the genre. The title of the Heart Sutra appears to refer to the use of perfect wisdom to cleanse error from the heart. There are numerous variations of the sutra in Sanskrit and many other classical Asian languages.

In Hawaii, *mana* (or energy) comes from water (or zwai) the ultimate source of life. In the Bible, it speaks of manna from heaven. The Hebrew word "man," pronounced *mawn*, means a whatness (so to speak). Manna in Hebrew means gift. In the Bible in Exodus 16:35 it states, "And the children of Israel did eat manna forty years, until they came to a land inhabited; they did eat manna until they came unto the borders of the Canaan." Manna from heaven in the Christian faith means food from heaven or spiritual food. In the New Testament of the Bible in Revelations 2:17, it reads, Jesus speaking, "He that hath an ear, let him hear what the Spirit says unto the churches. To him that overcometh I will give to eat of the hidden manna, and I will give him a white stone, and in the stone a new name written, which no man knoweth saving he that receives it." Could Jesus be speaking here of the heart life force energy or "L" energy? What is spiritual food?

"*Wai wai*" means being wealthy with plenty of energy; the Hawaiian word for heart is "puuwai," which means "lump of water," or life energy. Water is accountable for over two-thirds of our planet and also constitutes 99 percent of the body's molecules. Practitioners have discovered that water, along with everything in the cosmos, contains, receives, and sends subtle energy and has its own form of "liquid memory." Dr. Paul Pearsall, in his book *The Heart's Code,* states that there is a fifth force that he calls *"L" energy,* which travels at more than 186,000 miles per second, and accounts for "nonlocal" effects of occurrences; such as, remote healing and the power of intercessory prayer. The heart is uniquely composed of "L" energy and communicates and conveys it in its own form but is also "piggybacked" on the electromagnetic field (EMF) created by the heart. The heart's EMF is five thousand times more powerful than the electromagnetic field that is created by the brain and is subtle and has nonlocal effects that travel within these forms of energy. "L" energy also fills all of space in the form of bundles of vibrating energy that can manifest themselves either as particles or waves that contain the information transmitted within to all persons. Quantum physicists call this "wave-particle" duality principle associated with "L" energy.

In the following chapters we want to elaborate on the narrative process, which is a large part of the HeartPath process. Science has shown us that words are energy, and energy affects matter. Regarding the significance of words, John 1:1–4 says: "In the beginning was the Word, and the Word was with God, and the Word was God. The same was in the beginning with God. All things were made by him; and without him was not any thing made that was made. In him was life: and the life was the light of men." The words appear to carry vibrations of energy that affect the atoms that make up what we see around us. Scientists have also shown that the electron shown orbiting the nucleus is not always there in particle form. It exists in a wave state (like a cloud, everywhere at once) until someone looks at it. When the scientist observes it, it suddenly appears as a dot (particle). "How does it know someone is looking at it?" Charles Tart, physicist stated, "It is clearly responding to the observer's interaction with it."

Sacred Heart

In early Christian art in the Roman catacombs, there are many paintings of Moses striking the rock, which signified to the early Christians the crucifixion of Christ and the opening of his side. One may also see many drawings and early mosaics depicting the Lamb described in the Bible in Revelation 22:1: "And he shewed me a pure river of water of life, clear as crystal, proceeding out of the throne of God and of the Lamb." From whom does the river of the water of life flow? Looking at this scripture verse, we also need to consider John 7:38 (NKJV): "He that believe in me, as the scripture has said, out of his heart will flow rivers of living water." Jesus, speaking in this verse, calls us to the royal sanctuary of his heart and bids us to drink of the waters of eternal life. His heart is indeed the innermost sanctuary of that temple, which is his body. From the prophecy concerning the living water that flows from the interior of Christ, Saint John leads us finally to the piercing of the side and heart. Immediately after, Jesus reveals his heart as the source of living waters in John 7:37–38. It states in John 7:39: "But this spake he of the Spirit, which they that believe on him should receive: for the Holy Ghost was not yet given; because that Jesus was not yet glorified." The Roman soldiers at the time of the crucifixion of Jesus were trained to use their swords to pierce the heart to ensure death whereby they "pierced the heart of their foe."

Saint Bonaventure reflected a deep devotion to the sacred heart of Christ in his work *Itinerarium Mentis in Deum*, where he speaks of the goal of a perfect union of hearts between the Christian and God. He states that this can only be attained through a passionate love of Christ crucified. He wrote:

> The heart I have found is the heart of my King and Lord, of my Brother and Friend, the most loving Jesus . . . I say without hesitation that his heart is also mine. Since Christ is my head, how could that which belongs to my head not also belong to me? As the eyes of my bodily head are truly my own, so also is the heart of my spiritual Head. Oh what a blessed lot is mine to have one heart with Jesus . . . Having found this heart, both yours and mine, O most sweet Jesus, I will pray to you my God.

John Tauler was considered one of the greatest mystics and preachers and held a deep veneration for the Apostle John. He wrote the following as an example of his meditations on the piercing of Jesus' side:

> What more could he still do for us that he has not done? He has opened his very Heart to us, as the most secret chamber wherein to lead our soul, his chosen spouse. For it is his joy to be with us in silent stillness, and in peaceful silence to rest there with us. He gave us his Heart all wounded, that we may abide therein until we are wholly cleansed and without spot; until we are made like unto his Heart, and rendered fit and worthy to be led with him into the divine Heart of the Father. He gives us his Heart wholly and entirely, that it may be his dwelling place. He gives us his Heart as a resting place, dyed with the purple of his blood, adorned with red roses. In return he asks for our heart, decked with the white lilies of good works.

It was to Margaret Mary Alacoque in the 1600s, a humble Visitandine of the monastery at Paray-le Monial, that Christ chose to reveal the desires of his heart and to confide the task of imparting new life to the devotion.

On December 27, 1673, Margaret Mary had a vision that she describes as follows:

> Once, however, when I happened to have a little more time to myself than usual, and I was spending it in front of the Blessed Sacrament, God's presence seemed to envelop me completely. I forgot all about myself, and where I was, it was so intense; I simply gave myself up to the Spirit of God my heart, a willing prey to the violence of his love. For a long time he kept me leaning on his breast, while he revealed the wonders of his love

and the mysterious secrets of his Sacred Heart. Till then, he had always kept them hidden; but now, for the first time, he opened his Heart to me. The realistic and tangible way in which he did so, as well as the effects which his grace had on me, left no room for any doubt; still, I'm always afraid of being mistaken whenever I describe what goes on inside me.

What happed, I think, was this ... "My divine Heart," he told me, "is so passionately fond of the human race, and of you in particular, that it cannot keep back the pent-up flames of its burning charity any longer. They must burst out through you and reveal my Heart to the world, so as to enrich mankind with my precious treasures. I'm letting you see them now; and they include all the graces of sanctification needed to snatch men from the very brink of hell. You are the one I have chosen for this great scheme; you're so utterly unworthy and ignorant, it will be all my work."

Next he asked for my heart. I begged him to take it; he did and placed it in his own divine Heart. He let me see it there, a tiny atom being completely burned up in that fiery furnace. Then, lifting it out now a little heart shaped flame he put it back where he had found it. "There, my well-beloved," I heard him saying, "that's a precious proof of my love for you, hiding in your side a little spark from its hottest flames. That will be your heart from now on; it will burn you up to your very last breath; its intense heat will never diminish only blood-letting will cool it slightly. But I shall cast the shadow of my cross over your bleeding; so deeply, it will bring you more humiliation and suffering than relief. That is why I insist that you ask for this treatment in all simplicity; you will then be doing what you are told, as well as finding satisfaction in shedding your blood on the cross of humiliation. As a proof that the great grace I have just given you is not an illusion, but the basis of all those which I have still in store for you ... although I've closed the wound in your side, you will always feel the pain of it. And how have you been describing yourself up to the present: my slave? Well, now I'm giving you a new name: the beloved disciple of my Sacred Heart."

Heart of Intention

Affectivity is separate from cognition. The moral self-transcendence has to do in part with the development of feeling. The heart's reasons as feelings are the intentional responses to values. It is faith then, in the loving knowledge of God's love, which floods our hearts. Therefore, affective or psychic dialogue is a dimension of the conversion of the heart.

A statement made by a seven-year-old, which frames the essence of pure intention: "I will choose the faith sticker and place it on my heart. I need a heart sticker too so I can have more love; you told me I am loved."

> "For as a man thinketh in his heart so he is."
>
> —King Solomon

> "Faith is the function of the heart."
>
> —Mahatma Gandhi

The word "heart" defies definition and points beyond itself to mystery. It refers to the mystery of personal unity of the whole in the part and the part in the whole. The heart is a symbol since it causes and contains the reality of love it signifies.

> "For now we see through a glass, darkly; but then face to face: now I know in part; but then shall I know even as also I am known."
>
> 1 Corinthians 13:12

Various organized religions present as the path back to God, but many get lost at times in man-made rules and traditions. The scripture, which tells us we must worship God in spirit and in truth, can be lost within the social programs and marketing created to keep the church membership up. The heart releases the emotion of a strong desire to have a personal relationship to the one who loves us and created us for his pleasure. We, being as one with our heavenly Father God, find pleasure when we reconcile our heart and mind back to true self.

Pure Heart

> "When he left this life he left with his heart open and his eyes closed."
>
> —Author unknown

As we read with an open mind and a pure heart, we begin to understand that when we are born, we have our first experience of our physical body's existence and "breathe life." The divine spark within was already connected inside our mother's womb. Our heart memory of the spirit life with God is stored within our inner heart. Our first experience of separation happens when we are aware that our mother has walked away from us. She returns, but for that space in time, we don't know that she will.

As we grow and develop, our minds begin to adapt to our external environment while our emotions try to adapt to this strange world we find ourselves in. We experience dreams and visions, some of which by age four we are able to express. It is not unusual for children to report seeing Jesus in the sky or angels. It makes you wonder if the imaginary friends that children speak of are actually angels. Jesus says that where our heart is, there is our treasure (Matthew 6:26). The mind's ego gives us a treasure map that leads us to a pot of gold that is the cost of our soul to get. The heart begins to weep and constrict the flow of our lifeblood, affecting every area of our body.

The word "heart" in Aramaic is *leba* (Douglas-Klotz, 1999).

- This word in Aramaic means the center from which life radiates.
- Unselfishness and loving kindness to all beings is a way of purifying the heart.
- This purity of heart will bring the vision of God.

We grow and develop and experience relationships with others. The oneness that we felt with God before coming to this world begins to fade away. There is a deep desire in our soul to reconnect with something, but we don't always know what it is. We begin to attach to family, friends, and material things presented to us in this physical realm. The world does its best to wrap things up with pretty paper and shiny bows to keep our interest in earthly things. Nature cries out to try to remind us of who we really are and where we really come from.

Everything we see, from the changing seasons to the blooming flowers, reveals a life force of creation by a Creator that loves us. Even the great words of psalms in the Bible tell us that God knew us in our mother's womb (Psalm 139:13). The heart continues to try and pull the distracted mind back to things with meaning and purpose for our lives.

There needs to be an emphasis on affectivity as the center of our desire for God. The heart is the place where truth and love are unified. Martin Luther viewed the believing heart as clinging to God's word of grace. For John of the Cross, the heart is a religious symbol that both instructs and moves.

Native people use the image of the moist heart. Robert Bellah and other North American sociologists have written of "habits of the heart." Others may prefer to talk about desire, affectivity, union with God, or experiences of the Spirit. The experience of the Spirit is grasping an understanding that there is no separation from the love of God. The authors wish to reveal spiritual principles that support "the pure in heart shall see God."

Matthew 5:8 states, "Blessed are the pure in heart, for they shall see God." This scripture speaks to not just the heart but to our emotions, our mind, and our will; in other words, the whole person. Something so simple may have been overlooked since the beginning of the human race and caused many senseless divisions between the various denominations of the Christian religions, and all other world religions. When we begin to understand the way to connect our mind with our heart in unity, where the heart leads the mind, instead of the mind leading the heart, then we will find synchronicity that will lead us by intuition. Our thoughts connect to our emotions, which evoke a feeling that comes from our hearts and speaks to the heart of God.

Science and Religion

> "Science without religion is lame and religion without science is blind."
>
> —Albert Einstein

Research has shown that our feelings and thoughts have more control over our body's cellular functions than all the bacteria, viruses, and cholesterol in the world. The dilemma is based on the fact that the average human processes forty thousand thoughts and feelings each day. The question is, how do we monitor and make sense of our raging feelings and thoughts? The answer is to bring your thoughts, feelings, and actions into coherence with each other, a form of *reconciliation*. When thoughts, feelings, and actions are aligned and focused as one, we move from energy to matter and from illness to wellness in seconds.

We first need to have an understanding that we are energetic beings with an energy field that is electromagnetic. Science has shown us that every atom and subatomic particle has an energy field. The energy field of living organisms is constantly changing and is known as life force energy. Some would define this as energy or God, which are both fundamentally the same source with a beginning but no end. The earth is our realm of possibility. Intentions lead to thoughts, which lead to emotion. Thoughts can produce motion, and can affect the flow of God energy. Past memories or worry about the future also affects our spiritual energy. Memory is stored as an emotion picture, and memory is like a file system. Our goal should be to store positive emotional memory and release the negative.

The mind creates our reality, and so dysfunctional thought can cause a biochemical problem such as depression, anxiety, and mood disorders. We are the living thoughts of God, and those thoughts are energy. It states in the Bible that he is the Father of Light and we are the children of Light.

To begin a healing path, with the understanding of our energetic system of thought, we become aware that thoughts have the power to increase and decrease our flow of energy centered in the heart and traveling throughout our body. We must understand that our thoughts cause emotion and that our emotions will cause a change in our flow of spiritual energy when the emotion is negative and hurtful in nature. When we choose not to love or honor ourselves, the energetic system may become blocked. This may be why Jesus gave us the commandment to "love God with all of our soul, heart, and mind and to love each other as we love ourselves." Love is oneness with God who is love. Fear is the opposite and is an illusion of separation from God. Sin is also separation from God. Our flow of spiritual energy is connected to this oneness with God and all creation.

With an understanding that our thoughts are powerful, we must consider the importance of vision to maintain our focus and perseverance. In Habakkuk 2:2 it reads, "And the LORD answered me, and said, 'Write the vision, and make it plain upon tables, that he may run that readeth it.'"

By creating a vision board, one can keep one's thoughts on what one desires in one's life, for example, cutting out a picture of what one sees as one's ideal body weight. Telling yourself that you are overweight all the time will cause the energy to flow toward gaining more weight and feeling out of control. Resistance comes from thought. "What if I am wrong?" This statement equals fear. The greatest resistance we have is our fear. "What if this is true?" If we truly are in the presence of God, then we have a lot of work to do.

Our spirit is pure light and pure love, and the only time that our spirit is weakened is when the resistance connects to our fear. In Ezekiel 36:26 it says, "I will give you a new heart and put a new spirit within you; I will take the heart of stone out of your flesh and give you a heart of flesh."

Gregg Braden, former earth science expert describes the heart as a "seven-layered liquid crystal oscillator" that is responsible for tempering our understanding of the principles and stems from the logic of our thoughts from the left and right brain. This description of the heart is for those who are seeking a scientific definition and understanding of the heart. The heart is made up of seven alternating levels of muscle and has liquid crystal within its fluid content of the cells and the oscillator, which has the ability to tune into the electromagnetic pulse of the earth.

The HeartPath practitioner is always striving to help his or her clients develop a network to enable people to heal. Dr. Mikao Usui, Reiki Master, said it well in this way: "Just for today, I will let go of anger. Just for today, I will let go of worry. Just for today, I will count my many blessings. Just for today, I will do my work honestly. Just for today, I will be kind to every living thing."

Cardiovascular research has shown that entrained or smooth heart rhythm patterns can sometimes be seen when an individual does certain breathing exercises without focusing in the heart area or shifting emotional state. However, this approach imposes a pattern on the rhythms of the body instead of allowing the body's natural resonant rhythm to emerge. It is hard to maintain this coherent pattern for long without the heart losing focus and emotional shift. Focusing in the heart area will also produce an entrained or smooth heart rhythm pattern and is the best way to enter entrainment. It is the body's natural response to feeling good.

The use of self-biofeedback, such as HeartMath's Freeze-Frame, a computerized instrument that shows an individual his or her heartbeat, reveals that he or she has control, through heart meditation and breathing, to reach a smooth heart pattern. This is because the heart is a primary regulator of respiratory rhythm when we are relaxed. There are nerves that carry information from the heart to the respiratory centers in the brain, and this information regulates the start of the breathing cycle. By transcending and letting go of the mind's control of the breath, the body operates at its own resonant frequency. The goal is to get the mind out of the way so that the coherent, positive feelings are driving the process.

Pedagogic Experience/Healing Presence

The HeartPath practitioner has to be fully present with the individual who is describing his or her *lived experience* in a real way and to reflect upon the *pedagogic experience* that emerges from the dialogic conversation between the practitioner and client. The practitioner-client experience involves mood, emotions, energy, and feelings of relational quality that speak to the deeper understanding of the lived experience. The practitioner can then gently guide the client into a place where an individual's unique life story presents a healing presence and testimony.

The reflection of the told story produces a phenomenon of touching reality with the heart. There is a deep sense of inner peace knowing that with the realization of the presence of God, our divine source, we can be like a child again. The understanding of the love of God refines our hearts and provides a reflection of childlike invitation to him our eternal hope.

> "Be like a child, look at thy two feet and say Lord, walk these for me. Talk to him as to thy friend and nurse. Be in sweet common friendship with him. Call him in thy bath, in thy daily tasks, in thy going from one room to another. Say, Nay, I will not go

alone. Come, be thou with me, lead thou the way. Behold, he will answer then, and come running like laughter and golden hope into thy heart, and with understanding love will he walk with thee from room to room. And, too, will he stand beside thee when thou faceth thy friends and visitors, and he will place a hand in thine and will watch thy heart and the issues therefrom so that thou canst talk in perfect safety knowing that thy word will be food and drink and life to all in thy presence."

—Excerpt from Letters of the Scattered Brotherhood," Author Unknown

Chapter Four

Telling of the Story: A Journey to the Heart

"It is only with the heart that one sees rightly what is essential is invisible to the eye."

—Antoine de Saint Exupery

Words have meaning and power, as we clearly see when interacting with others in our life path. Whoever came up with the saying "Sticks and stones may break my bones, but words will never hurt me" spoke an untruth. Hurtful words spoken by various people in our past have a tendency to echo through our minds and try to define who we think we are. These words form thoughts and self-perceptions and, at times, take us away from our HeartPath to a path of doubt and a lack of forgiveness. The HeartPath practitioner always works from a relational stance and foundation.

The following excerpt from "The Essene Gospel of Peace," from the third century Aramaic manuscript and old Slavonic texts, talks about entering the sound of life.

And when the sun is high in the heavens, then shall you seek the Holy Stream of Sound. In the heat of noontide, all creatures are still and seek the shade; the angels of the Earthly Mother are silent for a space. Then it is that you shall let into your ears the Holy Stream of Sound, for it can only be heard in the silence. Think on the streams that are born in the desert after a sudden storm and the roaring sound of the waters as they rush past. Truly, this is the voice of God, if you did but know it. For as it is written, in the beginning was the Sound, and the Sound was with God, and the Sound was God. I tell you truly, when we are born, we enter the world with the sound of God in our ears, even the singing of the vast chorus of the sky, and the holy chant of the stars in their fixed rounds; it is the Holy Stream of Sound that traverses the vault of stars and crosses the endless kingdom of the Heavenly Father. It is ever in our ears, so do we hear it not. Listen for it, then, in the silence of noontide; bathe in it, and let the rhythm of the music of God beat in your ears until you are one with the Holy Stream of Sound. It was the Sound which formed the earth and the world, and brought forth the mountains, and set the stars in their thrones of glory in the highest heavens.

The HeartPath practitioner looks at the individual's inner heart and soul separate from the external reaction or behavior that causes the problem. When utilizing narrative techniques while viewing people as separate from the problem, the focus becomes to help people see problems as the product of circumstances or interpersonal processes. People are not the problem, but they are in a relationship with the problem. Our ongoing relationship with a problem creates an environment that either encourages it to thrive or to be diminished. It is possible to shrink, diminish, or eliminate the influence of a problem in our lives.

> "He made everything beautiful in its time; also he has made the world dear to man's heart, so that no man can find out the works which the Lord has done from the beginning to the end."
>
> —King Solomon, from Aramaic translation

Narrative Process

Human beings live by the meaning they attach to his or her story. It is in this way that we see a path unfold before us. It is in this way we discover our HeartPath. Our personal myths are powerful in that they forcefully shape our beliefs and convictions, thereby providing an active and dynamic influence on the future.

Human beings have many skills, competencies, beliefs, values, commitments, and abilities that will assist them. Narrative assessment sees the competencies of people and the beauty within as it seeks to build on personal strength instead of focusing on and correcting personal deficits. Narrative treatment demonstrates that human beings are motivated for positive transformation when immersed in such an emotionally safe environment.

Human beings also experience many ambiguities and contradictions in his or her self-narrative that may present in life as problems. Negative interpretations of events often have a negative effect. Problems are experienced as obstacles to a preferred way of being and thinking. They are the contradictions to one's preferred story. The HeartPath practitioner attempts to help the client make sense out of his or her life events to see the client's path as an opportunity to learn from life experiences and to reconcile these experiences to understand that God continues to reveal a personal path. What the client perceives to be an obstacle is looked at in a different light with the assistance of the HeartPath practitioner.

The HeartPath practitioner must be aware that narrative treatment does not support the role of expert in another person's life. The person consulting the practitioner is the true expert in regards to his or her own life. Narrative techniques require the practitioner to take a decentered, yet influential, position in the therapeutic relationship while maintaining a stance of curiosity or wonder. Of primary importance are the person's views, preferences, belief system, desires, hopes, dreams, and purposes. The narrative processing is a deliberate attempt to help people see their true story and step into their lives as a new reality, or a new way of looking at their realities.

The narrative technique approaches all people with honor and dignity. Some clients are unpleasant; they are challenging; they may have done miserable things; they may have physically or emotionally hurt others. You, as a HeartPath practitioner, must separate the behavior from the heart of the client. The HeartPath practitioner focuses his or her attention on the divine within each individual.

Focus on the individual's spirituality and connection with God so he or she can understand that forgiveness is available. This is part of the reconciliation process, and it seeks to provide an opportunity for God to help overpower and help the client overcome the problem.

The HeartPath practitioner also takes notice of the natural strengths and abilities the person has to stand against a negative or problematic influence. Helping the client see his or her path from the telling of his or her story, begins to see his or her testimony of God in his or her life and overcome many hard times he or she may express. Through a continued therapeutic conversation, the HeartPath practitioner seeks to reposition the client in relation to an issue that is of concern so that an individual might capitalize upon his or her natural strengths and make a conscious choice to re-author his or her story toward a preferred ending. As much as possible, the therapeutic power relation is minimized as the practitioner comes alongside the troubled client in a collaborative and interactive way.

Symbolic Meaning and Narrative

Repressed and/or suppressed memory tends to influence a neurologically wired process that perpetuates the stages of life. These states reflect early childhood experiences through lifespan experiences of life such as partner relations, marriage, middle age, senior citizenhood, and preparation for death.

For example, a young child feels little or no separation from the environment and especially none from the mother. The adult, however, completes the task of the ego development so that his or her boundaries can expand and make a way for self. This includes not only the full conscious self, but the personal unconscious and access to various symbolic images emerging from the collective unconscious. When Jesus asked us to come as little children, he understood that at any phase of life we are pure in heart, and we all have the ability to have complete trust in him every step of the way.

Narrative allows us to take a look at our symbolic themes and go through the process of illuminating our life path so that we can pursue healthy relationships. During guided imagery sessions you invite the client to discover symbolic themes, which many times are metaphoric of how he or she feels at this time in his or her life. As he or she discovers who he or she really is, he or she begins to understand the path that leads him or her up to this point in his or her life. This is healing in itself because it brings meaning to his or her story and understanding as to why certain life events happened and how he or she learned from them.

Narrative—Meaning-Making

> "Peace. It does not mean to be in a place where there is no noise, trouble, or hard work. It means to be in the midst of those things and still be calm in your heart."
>
> —Author unknown

Historically, the emphasis has been placed on observing outcome, specifically on how people cope following an event.

However, recent research appears to support the theory that perception, or meaning-making, is connected to memory through the processing of the lived experience. The various interplays lie between physiological, physical, sensory, social, behavioral, and spiritual, and tend to influence how we interpret or make sense of an event. Processing these lived experiences assists the individual in understanding his or her experience and facilitates storage of narrative memory.

Francine Shapiro, Ph.D., stated an individual could acquire numerous opportunities in therapy to reprocess his or her lived experience. He or she begins to understand his or her experience and the meaning that he or she attaches to it, resulting in the formulation of such experience. He or she also acquires the ability to generate profound meaning that can be further explored in therapy. If these theoretical foundations are true, then meaning-making needs to be processed in a way that supports the truth and meaning for the individual.

Narrative Approaches

Mental health practitioners are traditionally trained to research and analyze individuals with respect to an individual's normal and pathological characteristics. David Epstein, a narrative therapist, focused on developing an understanding of the cultural oppression and influence of a problem on an individual and the influence of an individual over the problem.

Self-report or open-ended questioning is repeatedly used to examine ongoing experiences in order to investigate social, psychological, and physiological processes relevant to day-to-day situations. A phenomenological study can explore a lived experience and conclude that the identification and insight into the individual's experience provided hidden meanings to emerge from the life narrative. For example, a recent study revealed profound insight for adult women who were exposed to partner abuse (McFeature, 2009).

In this study, ten women between the ages of twenty-five and fifty-five participated in an open-ended interview process. A narrative of each woman's experiences was co-created by the participant and the author. The individual's narrative was analyzed from a phenomenological perspective for the presence of common underlying themes unique to this sample. A pedagogic approach was utilized in an attempt to make interpretive sense of the phenomena experienced by the participants when sharing their stories. The result of the study was profound while revealing that the process of the "sharing of their stories" was extremely cathartic for them.

Story-based accounts termed narrative can be used to identify the experienced phenomenon. Life stories generated into narrative can provide insight into what it means to experience a life story and examine the subjective experience of meaning-making. A qualitative method of research is required in order to capture the human experience in search of meaning.

Michael Epston, a narrative theorist, also reiterated a statement over and over that identifies the narrative tradition in psychotherapy: the person is not the problem; the problem is the problem. Practical implications lead to the development of an array of ideas regarding types of questions that can be used to help the client externalize and deconstruct the problem. The client identifies outcomes toward a new story of his or her relationship to the problem. This therapeutic emphasis on working with the client's verbalized story of the problem and focusing on the therapeutic relationship itself is critical within narrative treatment. There may well be a first-order reality that exists independently of human attempts to know it. Individuals live in terms of a second-order reality that they actively construct. This line of thinking follows an integrative approach that pays attention to the client's story told through his or her healing journey. This narrative approach actively attempts to examine and restructure the client's story by working actively within the therapeutic relationship. Nevertheless, narrative therapists express the standards in narrative treatment approaches as: a) externalizing the problem; b) identifying preferred outcomes; c) identifying strengths and unique talents, and d) recruiting the client into an active and a collaborative effort to re-story.

An integrative perspective is accomplished by combining both humanistic life domains and constructivist narrative traditions that offer ways of identifying and working through ambivalence. This assists the client to move beyond his or her problem-saturated stories toward a more empowering narrative. This integrative perspective focuses on appreciating how the client's stories are lived in relation to the practitioner-client relationship. Gene Combs and Jill Freedman (1996) stated the client's narrative is lived within the therapeutic relationship, reflecting core themes that are clearly expressed in the client's verbalized stories. The client may not be focally aware until working with these lived stories, which can serve to enrich and facilitate the reconstruction process within narrative treatment.

People have used storytelling for centuries in order to convey values and exploration of life in general. In psychology, storytelling is an integral part of making sense of our lives. We achieve our personal identities and self-concepts through the use of narrative configuration. Our very existence and understanding as a whole is expressed in an unfolding and developing life story. The significance of an individual's subjective experience of his or her life story is a primary theme to engaging toward a journey of healing.

An individual can acquire numerous opportunities in therapy to reprocess his or her lived experience. He or she begins to understand his or her experience and the meaning that he or she attaches to it, resulting in the formulation of such experience and the ability to generate alternative meanings that can be explored in therapy. If these theoretical foundations are true, then meaning-making needs to be processed in a way that supports the truth and meaning for the individual.

There is an increased awareness of the impact of an individual's life story that includes the ebbs and flow of life with mixed emotions. There is also a noted increased compassion to reach others who are involved in the healing arts or feel that they have been called to the HeartPath to help others. We began to realize the significant importance and value in continued research that would reveal both objectively and subjectively an individual's lived experiences, leading to healing in the process of the "sharing of his or her story."

We hope to continue to learn and share with others the significant impact and application that our life narratives can reveal. In this book, we have attempted to show this phenomenon of healing as the HeartPath. As you work with your clients by honoring everything they share with the presence of reflective listening from a sacred heart, they begin to honor their life stories. They begin to understand that everything does happen for a deeper purpose. They begin to see through "spiritual eyes" that life is an "earth school." Each of us has an opportunity to give to those who come into our path, and this is the unity applied to our HeartPath.

Knowledge acquired from this book and our research will hopefully be of benefit to help professionals who work in the various healing arts, in addition to individuals that are prepared to assist others in their "call to serve others." The healing work begins in making sense and meaning out of difficult life events, such as relationships relevant to domestic violence, child abuse, divorce, loss and grief, and other life-changing milestones.

Core Themes

The purpose of identifying the client's unique and common core themes is to try to grasp the central meaning of each individual's reported lived experience. The processes of uncovering or recovering themes that are embodied in the narrative reflect the process of insightful discovery or exploration of his or her life journey. The approach to uncovering rich core theme material is to attend to the nonverbal or verbal dialogue as a whole and actively and compassionately listen to the revealed themes about his or her reported lived experiences.

There are core themes that clearly come out of the narrative process. Identifying the core common and unique themes is important for your client to be aware of. These core themes are universal and come into all of our life paths at some time in our life stories. Many times people will try to run from the reality of these sometimes painful themes. If they are not addressed, we may find ourselves turning to other ways of numbing the emotional pain or running from our own life in general. A single case study will be presented in chapter eight that will further explore these core themes.

People have used storytelling for centuries in order to convey individual values and exploration of life in general. Storytelling is an integral part of making sense of our lives. We achieve our personal identity and self-concept through the use of narrative configuration. Our very existence and understanding as a whole is expressed in an unfolding and developing life story. The client will begin to understand his or her lived experience and the meaning that he or she attaches to it resulting in formulation of such experience and ability to generate alternative and reconstructive meanings that can be explored within the healing process.

Chapter Five

The Phenomena of the HeartPath Experience

The aim of this chapter is to evaluate the client's reported lived experience and resulting emotional, mental, physical, and spiritual problems. Evaluating the phenomena of this process will help us to understand the importance of an individual's lived experience within interpersonal relationships that are relevant to each individual's life experiences. Daniel Siegel, M.D., stated this "joining process" occurs in both verbal and nonverbal responses that function as signals. Both responses are components of speech that contain information that create mental representational themes within the mind. These nonverbal signals (facial expressions, tone of voice, gestures, and timing of responses) have a direct impact on our socially related perceptions in the brain. The expression of these emotional elements or signals serves to activate the neuronal circuits that mediate attention, meaning, and arousal.

Phenomena of Understanding

The HeartPath practitioner involves an integral methodology that includes objective, subjective, and intersubjective approaches to understanding the human experience. Integrative health care practitioners—the doctors, nurses, and therapists—have opened themselves to an entire spectrum of consciousness matter to body to mind to soul to spirit and have thereby acknowledged what seems to be happening in any event. Body and mind and spirit are operating in self, culture, and nature, and thus health and healing, sickness and wholeness, are all bound up in a multidimensional tapestry that cannot be cut into without loss.

Martin Heidegger, a phenomenologist, stated that an important aspect of this approach is to listen and allow the text or narrative to speak to us. Heidegger also stated that: a) the responses are received between the dialogue of past and present; b) questions are asked from a historical vantage point; and c) the practitioner attempts to reconstruct the problems identified and reinterpreted his or her narrative through meaningful outcome. The present evaluation of the past reflecting a living continuity can only produce the phenomenon of understanding when our horizon of historical meanings and assumptions fuse with the horizon within the narrative itself. This fusion of horizons is represented by a more complete understanding of ourselves.

Phenomenological Narrative Research

Phenomenological research emphasizes the meaning of lived experience. Obtaining an individual's descriptions of experiences provides the practitioner with a better understanding of the deeper meaning and significance of his or her human experience.

Phenomenology is concerned with the phenomena that are given to experiencing individuals. This rigorous, descriptive approach offers a method for accessing the phenomena of human experience. The philosophical phenomenological method has three interlocking steps: *phenomenological reduction*, description, and narrative material seeking the most significant invariant meanings of a context, i.e., themes.

Phenomenology derives life themes from the phenomenon of consciousness and identifies the total coherence of an individual's lived experience. Consciousness makes its presence felt. Another term that may be applied is the *essence* of the phenomena. Consciousness contributes to the very meaning of objects (an individual's described narrative themes or patterns) by its very style and form.

The role of the practitioner is to study a described situation, experience, action, concept, and motive that focuses on the phenomena and reflects a structured ensemble of analysis. A sequential analysis of contextual material tries to understand how the participant interacts and develops his or her responses embedded into the narration. The participant's narrative has a connection between life autobiographies and horizons of past, present, and future concerns, relevant to context and structure of the phenomena.

The determination of the meaning or essence of a phenomenon is something everyone does constantly in everyday life. The insight into the essence of a phenomenon involves a process of reflectively appropriating, clarifying, and explicitly structuring the meaning of the lived experience. Human meaning can only be communicated textually by way of organized narrative. In order to grasp the meaning of the text, the practitioner seeks approachable ways in finding structures of meaning or themes. Focus is on the reflection of lived experiences and reflectively analyzing the structural or thematic aspects of that experience. Thematic analysis refers to the process of recovering the themes that are embodied and dramatized in the evolving meanings and imagery of the work. Thematic analysis is conducted by the practitioner in order to make sense of a text or lived experience by interpreting its meaning, which gives control and order to the constructed narrative.

The purpose of phenomenological reflection is trying to grasp the essential meaning of something. In order to grasp the structural meaning of a text, one must think of the phenomenon described in the text in terms of meaningful units on themes. Reflecting on lived experience then becomes reflectively analyzing the thematic aspects of that experience. This process is described as uncovering or recovering themes that are embodied in the evolving meanings and imagery of narrative text.

Making something of a text by reflecting a lived experience provides a more accurate meaning through a process of insightful discovery. Phenomenological themes may be understood as the containment of experience. For example, situational experiences were all gathered around a single case study involving a woman who reports exposure to multiple losses in close relationships. In other words, the practitioner tries to uncover something meaningful, reflecting deepened understandings of that notion. The phenomenological theme that is derived from the text is concepts, categories that are a component of the structure of a lived experience.

Thematic Material

Any lived-experience description is a source for uncovering thematic aspects of the phenomenon itself. Phenomenological analysis attends to the spoken language through thoughtful, reflective grasping of the client's verbalized words and practitioner's brief notes pertaining to nonverbal emotional cues. A phenomenological analysis of the client's profound sense of experience or meaning regarding one's belief in the world and awareness of one's subjective feelings and expectations are reflective of one's phenomenon of reported lived experience.

The life narrative, which was reported during the initial intake session, was used for the process relevant to the HeartPath. This told story was then interjected into a process throughout several healing sessions. The principles of heart memory, synchronicity, meaning-making, soul-searching, and faith-building all helped the client put together and make profound sense of his or her experience affecting the way that he or she think and look at his or her world.

Life narrative is a phenomenon in the universal world that is strictly correlated to the lived experience within life narrative and is identified as knowledge for any client who apprehends it. The goal of phenomenology is to arrive at a structural understanding of specific and concrete lived experiences by being fully and critically present to situations where the desired experiences take place, via co-creating between the practitioner and the client's reported lived experiences.

The practitioner's deep interest and need to question something is centered on our own ability to know. Practitioners of this nature adopt a phenomenological perspective in order to bring an illumination to the question itself, such as pedagogic investigation of the client's schemata to life in order to make sense of his or her lived experiences. From a phenomenological point of view, the practitioner's questions refer back to the client's life: "who they are," and what makes the practitioner write, read, and talk behind the telling of the client's story. The next step in reviewing the nature of a lived experience is best understood by capturing the phenomenon or lived experience of each client.

Thematic Reflection

Thematic analysis is a process of recovering structures of life meanings that are embodied and dramatized in the lived experience represented in the client's "told story." Thematic reflection has interpretive influence when it allows the practitioner to proceed with life theme descriptions. These descriptions represent the analyzed thematic meanings of the phenomenon or lived experience in question. These meanings reflect ways the practitioner will assist the client in making sense of reported life experiences.

Thematic analysis techniques are utilized in the construction of themes and patterns predominant in each client's told story. These techniques reflect a holistic approach relevant to each client's "telling of their story." Max van Manen, phenomenologist, utilizes selective highlighting and detailed (line-by-line) techniques by color coding the themes. The practitioner will also use effective observation and make notes relevant to the tone of voice, emotional reflection, and silence that tends to illuminate the very essence of the phenomenon or core themes.

The HeartPath sessions are interpretive conversations where a reflective orientation is the grounding that brings the significance of the client's life questions into view. The phenomenon of verbalized lived experience is grounded in exploring the structures of the human life domains as experienced in everyday situations and relations. The four life domains are mental, emotional, physical, and spiritual. These life domain themes are considered a guide for phenomenological questioning and reflect on the integration of other identified themes. The HeartPath practitioner will take a macro and micro approach to this thematic investigation of the narrative text. The practitioner will identify and categorize the data by color coding thematically and establishing a clear schematic or cognitive framework utilizing the life domain themes of the lived experience. The narrative text brings a *pedagogic experience* into a metaphorical and symbolic form that will present itself as a conversational relation between the practitioner and client.

The practitioner should be mindful of the question being asked, explored, and manifested, relevant to the meaning-making outcome that represents the telling of the client's story. The practitioner wants to become acquainted with the client's life domains. The practitioner should pay close attention to language—schemata (cognition of themes), what is being said or what is not said (silence). Speech rises out of silence, which becomes the client's verbalized life narrative constructed from conversational relation. A strong emphasis is placed on the participant's telling of the story, reflecting a rich, in-depth, and quality narrative.

The practitioner reflects a strong emotionality and vivid mental representations of the client's told story to feel the client's pain and energy throughout the initial intake and healing sessions. This process can make clear a visual, auditory, tactile, and olfactory sense of the client's reported lived experience. This holistic process requires an integrative mind-set and attachment between the practitioner and client, which truly constitutes and supports the term pedagogic reflection. A pedagogic reflection regarding the individual's telling of the story generates uniqueness and a strong relationship with decisions made and actions taken within the life narrative of the lived experience.

The practitioner must pay attention to both descriptive and interpretative expression in generating insights into the client's life narrative. The practitioner will attempt to organize the themes of the life narrative from a part-whole inquiry approach. The practitioner will reflect the process of life domains analysis, the identification of particular themes and patterns relevant to commonality, uniqueness, and life-journey perspectives.

Telling of the Story: Lived Experience is Therapeutic

When a person tells his or her life story, it becomes cathartic in itself. There are several things that occur during this process. The first is that he or she must trust you enough to share his or her story with you. When you reflect compassion, it is interesting to see that the trust comes quickly and may not take several sessions of rapport building. For example, hairdressers are probably more trusted than someone's identified best friend or therapist. This may be because the hairdresser is caring for a person's physical appearance. Another reason may be that people get so busy in their day-to-day life activities that sitting at the hairdresser may be the only time they slow down to think and talk about their day.

In the telling of the story there is also a feeling of release and letting go. For some it may be the first time of sharing his or her whole story. They may have been holding it in for many years and may even have felt somehow ashamed about what has happened to them. The HeartPath practitioner is just listening at this point and reflecting a presence of compassion. Mother Teresa stated that we should be "an expression of God's kindness." Kindness can be reflected in the process of taking time to listen.

An individual may also experience new insight as to how and what has happened to them based on issues relative to his or her current relationships. They may have an "aha" moment that may also be accompanied by a flood of emotions. The HeartPath practitioner continues to listen and encourage them to feel these emotions in a process of surrendering to the emotion.

The telling of a person's story also becomes therapeutic as the client begins to develop an understanding based on how he or she viewed him or herself, and what was important to him or her. An acknowledgement of how he or she changed and how he or she dealt with the lived experience itself also comes to his or her awareness. In the client's attempt to describe his or her lived experience of the issue at hand, relational issues, depression, anxiety, or other emotional stressors, he or she expresses details of life events that include who was involved and what he or she believed led up to these events. The client's experience may also reflect a more intense effort when describing his or her fears, grief, expressed guilt, self-destruction, inadequacies, deficiencies, and interpersonal relations with significant others.

The results of his or her telling of his or her story can be very significant to each client as he or she forms a description and understanding of his or her lived experience. The HeartPath practitioner will be able to piece together each client's identified themes, which always seem to capture his or her lived experience to form a life path with meaning. Both the content and process of each client's lived experience must be carefully received by the practitioner in order to capture the very essence and pedagogic meaning that portrays the client's experiences.

The engagement in phenomenological inquiry manifested the understanding between both the practitioner and client. The understanding is a life process in which a community of life is lived out. The practitioner should use guided questions that can facilitate and presumptively generate the wonder, details, struggles with "why" questions, and experiences of each client.

The HeartPath practitioner should give feedback to the client with a clear creation of ideas that support the essence of each client's unique lived experience within the precognitions of his or her life events, present events, and past events with his or her future hopes. In the assessment phase, the practitioner will use life domains, affective observation, and general thematic analysis. This information is gathered in order to generate meaningful themes and patterns, reflecting the uniqueness, similarities, and identified process recognition of past, present, and future. In addition, the impact of environmental factors suggests both similar and unique themes representing the client's lived experience.

The storytelling process presents a depiction of content (behaviors) reported by the clients, representing an objective component of his or her dialogue and transcribed narrative. Affective observations may represent an array of symptoms associated with feelings of self-disgust, grief, trauma effect, sense of stupidity on their part, lack of self-worth, and/or other painful thoughts. The practitioner, in his or her assessment, should describe in detail any commonality of themes that present with frequency and meaning, such as the essence of silence between the practitioner and participant. The importance and profound meaning that silence brings to an individual's language illuminates his or her very words themselves. The notion of the lived experience as an immediate awareness by the practitioner may be observed in silence. This practitioner will note silence within each client's narrative, reflecting this very phenomenon. The language can take the practitioner beyond the content and process of the metaphoric meaning where language speaks through silence.

Silence may be a portal to prompting the participant to share the "telling of their story." How conversational interviews tend to lapse into silence can be interpreted into a sense of fulfillment and closure. Silence by definition is the immediate nonverbal awareness by the practitioner that brings profound meaning to an individual's whole dialogue. The phenomenological inquiry requires that we as practitioners be pedagogically attentive to the essence of silence revolving around the content and process of the telling of a client's story. This will disclose a much deeper meaning of his or her world. The identified theme of silence can be quite evident throughout each narrative, being held with profound, deep meaning, reflecting a lack of closure, representing identified fear, anger, guilt, withdrawal and containment of emotions, and, in some cases, a sense of closure.

Subjective observations from the telling of the story can be expressed through a particular understanding. This understanding represents the development of behaviors and the client's gained awareness of how these behaviors can impact his or her own well-being, which they utilized in order to cope with relational issues.

Summary of the Purposes of Stories

Telling stories is sacred work and also multicultural work. Mary Elizabeth Mullino Moore, Professor of Theology and Christian Education, wrote that stories are an invitation to cross the boundaries of our worlds into the worlds of others, including cultural and religious traditions. Stories are also an invitation to cross the boundaries into our own depths and lived mystery.

Stories take clients deeper into themselves. Stories affirm the value of prior experiences. Stories connect clients' lives, issues, hopes, and fears with key course concepts and content. Stories honor and empower clients' voices, especially different student voices. Stories show the value of diversity and build learning communities. Stories connect people together in learning about each other. Stories help clients replace embedded images in the brain with new ones. Stories encode and structure memory for deep learning and making meaning. Stories become "texts," pedagogical representations that make connections visible and concrete. For all these reasons, telling stories enhances our healing process.

The use and power of stories is consistent with the growing body of literature on the role of emotions in learning and its inextricable connection with the intellect. It shows how the synergistic interplay of effect and cognition depends on replacing prior embedded mental images or on unlearning prior misconceptions and errors. The unlearning happens by moving from "neuronal networks" in the inner emotional centers of the brain (limbic cortex) to the more cognitive, integrative reasoning centers in the outer cortex. Deep learning, therefore, depends on the brain processing first emotionally and then making reasoned connections. Emotional experiences enhance critical thinking; mind, body, and feelings are all involved in a holistic process of learning.

Stories, along with music, metaphors, and memory, best help us access emotions. Stories engage all parts of the brain. Stories come from our experiences, our memories, our ideas, our actions, and our feelings. We should tell stories, create stories, and repeat stories.

A significant part of the Bible is devoted to narrative literature, also referred to as "story." Advantages to focus on within the stories include intrinsic interest involved in the stories, the patterned nature of the stories, the timeless truths illustrated, and the way the stories lend themselves to easy application.

Nearly one-third of the Bible is narrative. Following the story line can facilitate a grasp of some of the characteristics of narrative. A narrative, in its encompassing sense, is an account of events and participants moving over time and space, a recital with a beginning and ending. The features of narrative are best preserved by preaching narrative, as God gave them, in story form.

For example, the preacher must move in and out of the story with analogues, explanations, and interpretations as the plot line of the story moves along. The expositor may simplify a potentially complex task of representing patterns and preserve the narrative's patterned quality most effectively. Narrative is timeless and universal. One of the best formats for bringing out either the narrative's timeless and universal character or its redemption-historical development is the story-line sermon. Preaching narrative may at times sound historical. The preacher must move persons to identify with and live by the truth of the story. Stories may impact its audience in subtle ways by generating emotions and feelings.

The easiest way to preach narratives might be to just retell the story, allowing the story itself to heighten points of application. A person's testimony is also very powerful and can be used in either individual healing sessions or in group work.

> Spring is a perfect time to join the growing number of people on the planet who are shifting their priorities to things that really matter. The happiest, most peaceful, most productive people we know have one thing in common. They may not be rich or highly educated, but they maintain laser-sharp focus on their priorities, which helped them transition from the materialistic world of excess and self-indulgence, the hallmark of our times, to the invisible realms of community action and service. To the great spiritual teachers, Peace, Love, Compassion, Forgiveness and Gratitude were not ordinary words; they were powerful Weapons of Mass Transformation.
>
> —Arntz, Hoffman, Chasse, Vicent, 2005

Endless Story

The endless story begins with each new life born into this world. The *gnostics* call this a soul falling down into a body. Jesus taught us about the gift of eternal life through him to our Father in heaven. Mankind is now facing a new life in a new world wired to reconcile to the Spirit of God. In seeking this union, there are lessons and stories weaving their way throughout the universe of synchronicity. Everything has a cause and effect, and everything affects everything else. The illusion of being separated from God is what keeps everyone searching, but it also places us at risk of being further divided. If you ask someone to write down his or her life story, it is interesting that it all revolves around relationships. We are social creatures. If one can see the connection and the lessons learned from these encounters, one would begin to see a path that is forming before him or her. The stories all have meaning and purpose, the stories remain alive and endless, but for some reason we don't always pay attention to the meaning and purpose of our lives.

Mother Teresa's life story is one of many stories that validate the meaning of the endless story. Mother Teresa, in her own words, often reminded people during the trials of life of a loving God in Scripture and the importance of prayer and sacrifice.

> "I will not forget you …
> I have graven you on the palms of my hands …
> I have called you by name …
> You are mine …
> You are precious to Me …
> I love you."
>
> —Based on Isaiah 49:16, Isaiah 43:1, 4

> Prayer enlarges the heart until it is capable of containing God's gift of Himself. Ask and seek and your heart will grow big enough to receive Him and keep Him as your own.
>
> —Mother Teresa

Chapter Six
HeartPath Principles

I open the doors of my heart wide knowing that the everlasting fountain of Thy light will pour forth and fill my life. I will be vigilant in guarding these doors that they shall not close of themselves because of my forgetfulness. I rest here with my heart open to receive, knowing that I am in the center of all things. I rest in gratitude and thanksgiving that the Spirit has filled this heart as a spring to break open and pour forth into my world. I will not let my heart be gripped by alarms and fears; it shall not be shut by violence nor any untoward event. My sole intent is to keep these doors open for my very life's sake, for I believe that out of the issues of my heart I shall be guided upon my journey and I shall be given strength.

—Sir Philip Sidney, 1554–1586

Scientific Research Regarding the Mind-Heart Connection

For many years, the mind was thought to exist within the confines of the brain. Scientists theorized that all of the information that we gained and retained was stored in the brain within the mind. Throughout history, people believed that love comes from the heart, and poets still pay homage to this notion. Surprisingly, the latest science shows that this idea may be based in reality. The function of the heart does affect the mind and emotions, possibly even more than the hormone-producing endocrine system, which is sometimes referred to as the "second brain."

Most fascinating of all, practitioners discovered that the heart-brain has the power to send messages to the brain. The messages are sent via the spinal cord and through the largest nerve in the body, the vagus nerve, which stretches from the brain to the torso. The vagus nerve is the longest of the cranial nerve. Its name is derived from Latin meaning "wandering." True to its name, the vagus nerve wanders from the brain stem through organs in the neck, thorax, and abdomen. Therefore, it's outdated to think that nerve messages travel only from head to heart: it's a two-way street. Because the heart can "speak" to the brain through the vagus nerve and spinal cord feedback system, it sometimes overrides messages that come from the brain, particularly messages of distress, which can trigger heart attacks.

As practitioners continued to study the surprising autonomy of the heart, which was previously considered by most scientists to be just a simple pump, they found that the heart is also an endocrine gland, which secretes its own hormone, ANF (atrial natriuretic factor). ANF influences not only the blood vessels and kidneys, but also the mood-influencing adrenal glands and the brain.

In the brain, parasympathetic (rest and digest responses that do not require immediate responses) or sympathetic (fight or flight situations that require immediate responses) impulses coming from the heart help trigger the onset of either calming or excitatory thoughts. This may be the reason why some heart transplant patients occasionally adopt personality tendencies of their donors, a phenomenon that has been noted since the beginning of heart transplantation.

In emotionally healthy people, there appears to be a strong tendency for the heart and brain to cofunction and to remain in synchronization or entrainment, which defines an experience of two events that are causally unrelated occurring together in a meaningful manner. Entrainment appears not only to reflect a positive frame of mind but also to help create it, in part by enhancing the balance of the autonomic nervous system. The body, clearly, can help heal the mind. But what inaugurates this healing? The mind itself! Your mind, when focused on appreciation, has an unparalleled power to trigger physical and emotional healing.

The power of the heart to influence the mind and emotions was first examined scientifically in the early 1990s. Initially these practitioners were intrigued by the fact that transplanted hearts are able to beat immediately upon transplantation, even before nerves coming from the brain are functional. This occurs, they discovered, because the heart has an intrinsic nervous system of its own, which can cause it to beat even without messages from the brain. This nervous system consists of masses of nerve cells, or neurons, similar to those in the brain. These masses of neurons include parasympathetic and sympathetic neurons that make heartbeat possible: contract, relax, contract, relax. Without them, the heart cannot function. This nervous system has been dubbed the heart-brain.

In this world of technology, the mind has obtained more ego control while the function of the heart is being neglected. Depression, suicide, anxiety, heart attacks, and other mental and physical health problems are all escalating. The mind continues to tell mankind that we are on the brink of new discoveries to heal these diseases and cure depression and the common cold with medications. We continue to fall into the trap of finding a pill for everything with the side effects worse than what we are trying to cure. There is too much good information now available for us to understand prevention than to allow physical heart health and mental health problems to prevail.

Heart Memory

Have you ever walked into a room and smelled some home cooking that brought back memories of your mom or your grandmother? The smell alone takes you to a place and time in your mind filled with childhood memories. Have you ever heard a song that reminded you of a place in time with your friends or your significant other? The song has a way of transporting you back to a time and place so many years ago that you probably haven't thought about until you heard the song. What about seeing something that they don't make anymore and being immediately transported to that space in time as if it were yesterday? You taste something like a piece of gum that you chewed during a special date with someone in high school. That taste takes you back to the date, along with all the details—the movie you watched, the temperature outside, what you wore. What about a dream of someone who is walking and talking with you and you awake expecting him or her to be there, but he or she died years ago? These are all examples of heart memory.

Heart memory takes you beyond a thought of a past event. Heart memory brings together all the senses, even the unconscious mind, and transports you to that time and place. Heart memory is no respecter of time, happiness or sadness, person, place, or thing.

Cellular consciousness is the ability to communicate desires and needs. The heart cell has the ability to communicate what it needs, such as oxygen, which is a biochemical feedback system. Every cell is new every six to nine months. The healing path understands the importance of awareness of thoughts, which cause energy and will result in a physical response.

According to Dr. Paul Pearsall, all living things are made of cells with trillions of tiny tuning forks, which resonate together by the energy of the heart; the cells reverberate in a concert of energetic harmony. *Cardio-energetics* suggests that this cellular symphony, including the billions of brain cells, constitutes a dynamic, systemic memory system that is, in fact, constantly vibrating with other memory systems that share and create info-energetic memories of our lives.

The heart, with its powerful, energized heart muscle fibers, coordinates not only our individual cellular symphony, but plays in duets with all hearts, persons, places, and things. Heart memory is a critical component that makes up who we are and how we have come to understand our life now, in the past and in the future. Heart memory appears to manifest from all senses: smell, taste, hearing, seeing, and touching.

HeartPath Narrative Process

Narrative techniques hold a strong conviction that human beings are meaning makers. Michael White clarified this foundational premise: "This is to propose that human beings are interpreting beings—that we are active in the interpretation of our experiences as we live our lives." Through lived experiences, we strive to make sense of our world and our selves in order to find purpose and direction in the context of our own living. Although people tend to evaluate their lives on many different dimensions, meaning is often described in popular psychology as "happy, satisfied, fully functional, self-actualized, fulfilled, well adjusted, mature, free of anxiety, liberated, enlightened, individuated, and saved."

Human beings are arrangers. As active participants in the interpretation of our lived experience, we arrange life events into sequences across time in order to establish a coherent account of who we are—our identity. White proposed that "it is not possible for us to interpret our experience without access to some frame of intelligibility, one that provides a context for our experience, one that makes the attribution of meaning possible." Narrative in this frame of intelligibility and our particular arrangements of life events makes up our story, self-narrative, or personal myth. Dan P. McAdams believes this arranging is a natural human construction made in "an effort to bring together the different parts of ourselves and our lives into a purposeful and convincing whole."

Methods of Practice

When people first turn to a practitioner, they often start by the telling of their story about their lives and a problem that they are experiencing. The HeartPath practitioner understands the power of the client feeling safe to share his or her story to someone who is bound to confidentiality and is listening with compassion. These life stories are, most of the time, problem-saturated accounts of confusion, frustration, and worry that over time have become the dominant plot of a person's life story as more and more attention gets focused there. There is a firm acknowledgment that there is more to this map or the client's story that has not yet been highlighted. The problem is part of the client but not all of the client. It is further contended that mental representations allow the complexities and contradictions of life to reflect movement. The mental representations often consist of a judgment on a person's actions and identities. These mental representations communicate weakness, disability, dysfunction, or inadequacy. They create a sense of being stuck.

As the problem-saturated story is repeated over and over again, it gets bigger, all the while gaining more power to negatively influence the future. This also begins to form a negative cycle of thought processes that becomes a *contamination cycle*. A cycle of contamination is associated with ruminating thinking of negative thoughts, and results in a person stuck in this cycle. This contamination cycle has the potential to take a person down a path of self-destruction.

The HeartPath practitioner, through narrative-based techniques, will ask questions of the client in order to facilitate a rich description of the problem. They are interested in his or her life or history of a problem and how it has been creating an effect on the person. Rich description requires detail and expanded accounts of the life of problems. As this in-depth description unfolds, the practitioner catches a glimpse of the problem's personality, its tricks, tactics, way of operating, rules, motives, plan, allies, and intentions.

The focus should be on the intentions of the client as well as what he or she perceives to be the intentions of the other person in the relationship. Many times the client will begin to see a pattern of behavior by a significant other and ask him or herself the question, "What are his/her intentions?" Intentions come from the heart, which then motivate a person's thoughts and actions.

The HeartPath practitioner looks for opportunities to invite the client to give a specific name to the problem through a word or a short phrase. This process is known as naming. Naming is an excellent tool for externalizing problems or shifting the problem from inside the person to outside the person while separating the person's identity from the problem. Immediately the person comes to understand that this something with a name is something other than self. The door is now open for externalizing conversations. This is critical, especially when dealing with a client who internalizes his or her anxiety and/or depression.

Externalizing Conversations

Externalizing conversations are conversational exchanges where the practitioner purposefully uses language embodying an implicit assumption that the problem is having an effect on the person rather than existing within them. These types of conversations are linguistic devices, in that they create a shift in understanding of who the person is and where the problem resides.

We believe the framework (story) and the language (externalizing conversation) of narrative psychology and the HeartPath is consistent with the framework (parable) and the language (standing against negative influence) demonstrated in the life of Christ. Jesus used his life to help others see the possibilities of overcoming negative spiritual influences and thereby moving them into a meaningful existence. "Thou mayest" became possible because God's grace is at work in and through us. We can be overcomers.

Alice Morgan, a narrative therapist, explained, "When people are separated from the problems, their skills, abilities, interests, competencies and commitments become more visible. The more visible these skills become, the more available they are for people to access." Externalizing conversations reduce guilt and blame yet leave room for responsibility. This shift in understanding is critical to the narrative technique.

Human beings commonly practice internalizing conversations, assuming the problem is somehow within them. Externalizing conversation releases people from the burden of being the problem, thus creating options and the possibility of working cooperatively to revise a relationship with the problem or to take action against that which contradicts one's preferred way of being and thinking.

When considering the life of problems, narrative techniques underscore the importance of understanding that problems can only survive and thrive in an environment that nurtures them. One must discover, acknowledge, and deconstruct (pull apart and examine) the beliefs, ideas, and practices of the broader culture that encourage the life of a problem and thus contribute to the problem story. The environment in which a problem thrives is considered the context of the problem. People do not live their lives in a vacuum. People live in real worlds with cultural, social, spiritual, and political factors that complicate their story.

For example, Christ's life journey speaks to "His name is Emmanuel, God with us." Therefore, externalizing conversations, with conviction of "who I really am," creates a shift in thinking and being that greatly resembles the way Christ interacted with others. It is also important to understand "self" differently and to be able to see the other person from a different perspective as well. Joining with the client is a "gift of grace" that comes to us through the example and presence of God with us and in our hearts. Helping others join together is a gift to be given to all humanity.

God willingly entered the human story to be one of us. God's was a humble birth and a lowly life spent walking amongst the people. Jesus' main focus of ministry during his time on earth was an intimate closeness with ordinary people, transforming each individual's perspective on the positive importance of their life and how it has a place on the story of human history and on the story of God. Jesus cast out demons and negative influences that plagued the human creatures he knew to be otherwise beautiful and competent. He spoke powerfully against that which was destroying the human potential to actively and positively participate with God the Father. Jesus repeatedly demonstrated that, by the grace of God, new positions are possible in relation to problems, lives can be changed, and new direction can be realized. He brought hope, and he continues to bring hope.

Lowly and ordinary people came to believe their lives could have meaning and great purpose. People draw close to those who can demonstrate this positive understanding of the human condition through word and action. They begin to imagine the life they prefer and to believe in the possibility of achieving it. They make way for positive transformation. Jesus' life created a safe environment of great compassion for people to see and act on this positive choice or position.

Power-based relationships are especially influential. It affirms that it is important to "recognize that persons sometimes describe the distressing and unjust results of these social factors to themselves, as personal failures, shortcomings or faults, and that they are implicitly encouraged to do so by those who hold power" (Morgan, 2000). These types of power relations are continuously examined in narrative processes in order to give an accurate description of the problem and to find meaningful ways to stand against the root of trouble. A client's spiritual belief system is critical in this arena. It is important for the client to understand who he or she is in Christ/God. Power relations are continuously examined in order to give an accurate description of the problem and to find meaningful ways to stand against the root of trouble.

Reauthoring or restoring is the possibility of revising the relationship between the person and the problem. The focus is not on solving the problem; it is on exploring the problem. It is on exploring through the dialogue of the client his or her unknown possibilities within him or herself and his or her unseen life journey. Michael White refers to this process as the reauthoring of an individual's life story.

For a person to determine his or her own wishes, it is important to trace the history of the problem or the influence it has had over a long period of time. The HealthPath practitioner may have to remind the client that things did not happen overnight and therefore to be patient and give him or herself grace as he or she addresses the problem. It is also important to ask the client when he or she first noticed the problem, what was life like prior to the problem, and when the problem was the strongest or the weakest, or the problem's relative influence over an extended period of time.

Relative-influence questioning measures the strength of the problem and the strength of the client to stand against the problem over time. Of course, the problem may revolve around relationships and/or loss in his or her life. Mapping the relative influences of person and problem, then describing the effects on a life, helps clarify the impact of the dominant problem-saturated story. These conversations are powerful acknowledgments and help to reduce the sense of isolation. Morgan reminds us:

> When the problem is placed in a context over time, it is seen as changing and less static or fixed. Moments of greater or lesser influence can be identified. People often feel relieved to discover that the problem has changed at different times in their lives. When times of lesser and greater influence are discovered, new or different stories may emerge. As soon as these conversations are taking place, re-storying work has then begun.

Alternative story or unique outcomes are stories that stand outside the dominant story or problem and highlight times when the person was able to cope or manage in the face of the problem. In these stories, the problem had less or no influence while the person's natural strengths, skills, and abilities are shown to have a positive impact. Morgan describes it beautifully: "A unique outcome can be anything that the problem would not like." The person has mentioned aspects of his or her experience that appear to deny, contradict, or modify his or her dominant problem-saturated story, then the practitioner, through questioning, must invite the client to expand on the circumstances and nature of these unique outcomes and help the client focus his or her attention on how these do not fit with the story as told.

Unique outcomes demonstrate that the problem is never one hundred percent successful. Unique outcomes become sparking events that pave the way to new and different conversations that avoid thin conclusions. The HeartPath practitioner uses a landscape of action questions in order to provide a rich description of the client's unique outcomes by focusing on who, what, where, when, and how these exceptions took place, as well as a landscape of meaningful questions that explore the more positive events and the effect on the person. This technique continues to help the client see his or her life as a journey with experiences that bridge his or her path to what God has in mind for him or her. If the life experience or challenge appears to be a test, then it probably is.

Unique outcomes also assist in mapping the story for an individual to participate in this mapping of his or her personal path. The HeartPath practitioner will attempt to assist the client to trace his or her history and the effect of the unique outcomes on his or her life. These may become his or her testimony to him or herself and to others who have experienced similar life events or challenges. This can be his or her turning point. This is where he or she comes to the fork in the road of his or her path and either decides to remain in the problem-saturated story or to reposition him or herself differently in relation to the problem.

The HeartPath practitioner explores with the client the possible outcomes of these two different courses of action and paths with questions such as, "Where will this problem take you?" "What designs does it have for your life?" "How could the story change if you reposition yourself and act against the problem?" "What ending do you want to your story?" "Who would support you in your choice of positive action?" "Whose presence would empower you for such a change in direction?"

Throughout this narrative therapeutic process, the client has been ultimately invited to explore his or her landscape of identity, how he or she wishes to be identified or defined in life. This process helps lead a person into a place where he or she expresses his or her preferred way of being by articulating his or her desires, wishes, preferences, personal values, personal skills, and abilities, as well as articulating his or her intentions, motives, plans, and purpose. The HeartPath practitioner is committed to the possibility of a new story to define the client and help him or her understand the purpose and meaning of his or her life path. The narrative technique provides a transformative process by allowing the client to see meaning in all his or her life experiences, both good and bad, as he or she perceives them.

The reincorporation metaphor is a process of assisting the client to rejoin with others in a familiar social world and encourages the recruitment of others in the celebration and acknowledgment of the person's arrival at a preferred destination or status in life. Stephen Arterburn, author and licensed minister, stated that healing is a choice, and there is a process for reaching a place of healing. These decisions will transform a person's life and help him or her understand that there are many lies that may prevent him or her from moving into healing.

The first choice is for the person to connect his or her life with others who will encourage him or her to move forward in his or her life. The lie that is often told to him or her is that all they need to heal is just God and him or herself. This will, many times, isolate the client from others as he or she attempts to heal alone, which often keeps him or her in a place of denial of any problems.

The second choice is to feel his or her life. We know that many clients will attempt to mask their pain with drugs and/or alcohol or other addictions to fill a void in his or her life. The lie that is often told to them is that real Christians should have a real peace in all circumstances. This lie often causes the individual to internalize to keep up a good image when around other professed Christians.

The third choice is the client's choice to investigate his or her life search for truth. The lie is that it does no good to look back or to look inside.

The fourth choice is to heal his or her future. The lie is that time heals all wounds. We understand that time does heal some in the process of grieving; however, the wound is not completely healed in the process of time alone.

The fifth choice is a choice for the client to help his or her life by seeking professional help. The lie is that a person can figure out things by him or herself.

The sixth choice is for an individual to embrace his or her life. The lie is that if he or she acts as if there is no problem, it will finally go away.

The seventh choice is the choice to forgive others and to forgive ourselves. The big lie is that forgiveness is only for those who deserve it or who earn it.

The eighth choice is a choice to risk your life. This may be the client's choice to enter into other relationships when a previous relationship has caused pain. The big lie is that a person must protect him or herself from feeling any emotional pain.

The ninth choice is to choose to serve others. The lie is that a person should not serve until he or she is completely healed and strong; there is no place for the person to serve God until then. Healing and renewed minds come from helping others.

The tenth choice is a choice to persevere. The lie is that there is no hope for the person. Perseverance comes from within and from the strength that only God can give us.

When the client begins the process of reauthoring, he or she must be open to the healing process and not buy into the lies that people may tell him or her, not realizing the harm of these lies. Reauthoring decisions may be documented through letters or rituals, such as journaling, in order to assist the client in reclaiming his or her life from the influence of the stated problems. Audiences or important supporting people are called upon to witness a personal testimony of this new direction or revised story of life. Remembering is an extension of this outsider witnessing, where supportive people who have been lost through death or distance are metaphorically invited to rejoin the supporting cloud of witnesses. Hebrews 12:1–2 considers our race of faith:

> Wherefore seeing we also are compassed about with so great a cloud of witnesses, let us lay aside every weight, and the sin which doth so easily beset us, and let us run with patience the race that is set before us, Looking unto Jesus, the Author and Finisher of our faith, Who for the joy that

> was set before him endured the cross, despising the shame, and is set down at the right hand of the throne of God.

Reflection of Our Life Path

> "The greatest science in the world, in heaven and on earth, is love."
>
> —Mother Teresa

As we all reflect on our life path, we can understand why it is so important to understand and place meaning to difficult and challenging life events. We begin to open up to the possibility of articulation of wounds that have served to either help us grow as individuals or have served to obscure our true identities. It is hoped that the path that unfolds will be one of understanding our true identity and lead us to an understanding of our spiritual life. The narrative principle of externalizing conversation is the form of release and acknowledgment that we can share our story and that it will be a testimony for someone who may also be experiencing similar life struggles. It becomes the path to who we really are.

The narrative process of reflection of our life path helps us to remember. When someone is struggling with a low self-image, it can be confusing when he or she sings of being the child of a King and then in another church hymn declares him or herself to be "a worm." When an individual feels belittled by the disappointment and judgment of others in a faith system that emphasizes our human carnal nature and yet points out the fundamental importance of purity, the individual may be confused and lost in the process. He or she may cry out within, "You don't know who I really am, and you do not see the beauty inside of me." Who we are should remind us that humanity is God's highest work of art, and we are created in God's image. The world would strive to steal this concept away and take us down a false path of destruction.

Who we really are should speak to understanding the life of problems. It should remind us that we are not the problem. We need to understand that the problem is the problem. Reflection on who we really are should remind us that God is by our side, supporting us, loving us, and fully aware of where we are and the unique challenges that we face. Who we really are should illuminate our paths and a realization that there is a new love for that glittering instrument, the human soul.

As we see our life path unfold, we may come to a fork in the path. This illustration may be shared with your client in a drawing showing the fork in the road and a decision to be made. This is based on the client's sharing how they see the two paths and what they each represent. A quote from a poem entitled "A Fork in the Road" may give new meaning to arriving at a place of decision-making at the fork in the road of our life path: "You see another fork in the road, to the left is history repeating itself, to the right is a new beginning" (Cinthia McFeature, "A Fork in the Road").

Science of Compassion

> "I believe the purpose of all major religious traditions is not to construct big temples on the

> outside, but to create temples of goodness and compassion inside, in our hearts"
>
> —Dalai Lama

The HeartPath practitioner seeks the heart of the Divine in order to express intentional compassion. This process for intentional compassion differs from *Webster's Dictionary* definition of compassion, which states that "compassion is a sympathetic consciousness of others' distress together with a desire to alleviate it." Intentional compassion is the intention to become compassion.

Human beings have many skills, competencies, beliefs, values, commitments, and abilities that will assist them, and the HeartPath practitioner recognizes the competencies of people. They see the beauty within as it seeks to build on personal strength instead of focusing on and attempting to correct personal deficits. The HeartPath will demonstrate that human beings are motivated for positive transformation when immersed in an emotionally safe environment.

Brain research utilizing functional magnetic resonance imaging (fMRI) has shown that manifestation of compassion and kindness through utilization of meditation practices affect regions of the brain. The fMRI shows that the detected emotions and feeling were significantly changed during these practices. These studies have verified the external impact a "compassionate intention" has upon an individual's ability to be empathetic to other individuals' well-being. Within the healing arts, a familiar theme is threaded throughout preventive health care as well as treatment and is highly valued. The practitioner creates a healing environment that focuses on an individual's internal state of mind and his or her external state of mind integrated to create a compassionate healing intention. Special focus is placed on describing a client's core themes, which is in direct response to every compassionate, healing intention and begins with the HeartPath practitioner. The concept of compassion and an accepting relationship with self is critical to creating a healing intention.

Compassion is a way to connect to the client's suffering journey and is co-created with the practitioner. This connection explores deep within the client's heart where emotional connections have caused much pain and stagnation in his or her life journey. The practitioner seeks a place of presence within a healing relationship in order to assist the client in creating a compassioned healing attitude. In this way the practitioner approaches the client's wholeness and well-being. A healing attitude requires viewing the inner self through heartfelt lived experiences and a nonjudgmental, compassionate process that allows the client to connect to each of the domains of his or her physical self, emotional self, mental self, and spiritual self experiences. These lived experiences are unconditional, ego-devaluated, and nonjudgmental, allowing the client to perceive his or her internal and external worlds with benevolence and with an open-heart process.

According to Gregg Braden and his lecture entitled "Beyond Zero Point," the science of compassion is our lifetime goal. Jesus was an "Essene Master," as he mastered his focus on forgiveness and compassion. Many scriptures in the Bible reflect his words on forgiveness and compassion. Mother Teresa was another example of someone who had mastered compassion. In order to be a committed HeartPath practitioner, one must become a *compassionate warrior*. We can begin to look at our thoughts without attachment to the outcome, our feelings without distortion of the feeling, and our emotions without charge or judgment. This path is one that does not allow for division of human beings at any level. This is the path that Jesus spoke of when he said in Matthew 18:4–5, "Whosoever therefore shall humble himself as this little child, the same is greatest in the kingdom of heaven. And whoso shall receive one such little child in my name receiveth me."

The science of compassion was based on a series of codes taken from the Dead Sea Scrolls, which were discovered in 1947. The compilation of these five codes that describe the mastery of compassion should be considered by the HeartPath practitioner. What opens us up to the process of compassion is a quality of thought, feeling, and emotion, which Jesus spoke of throughout his journey (Braden, 1998). The Essenes have five codes that were written 2,500 years ago that state how an individual thinks and emotes about these five possibilities is the process to becoming compassionate. This is a process for intentional compassion, which differs from *Webster's Dictionary* definition that "compassion is a sympathetic consciousness of others' distress together with a desire to alleviate it." As reflected in Jesus' life, compassion is a state of being and it is intentional. Jesus taught compassion as a way of life as he became compassion.

The Essenes taught that if we acknowledge, trust,

and believe in the following, we can become intentional compassion: 1) If we believe that there is a single source of everything—all that is and all that will ever be, and believe that every life event is a part of that single creative force, then we have mastered this first code. 2) Do you trust in divine timing? Do you trust in divine order? 3) Believe that every experience, without exception, is an opportunity to demonstrate mastery of this code. 4) Believe that your life mirrors your quest to know yourself in all ways. 5) If you truly believe that life essence is eternal, then the same may also apply to our whole being, resurrection. Our bodies are changing because the earth is changing, and therefore this is a part of the path. In order to help others come to a place of peace and reconciliation of these truths, we as practitioners must work on mastery of these so that we can become a living example of compassion. A practitioner is not called to judge people but to listen and reflect back compassion to allow the healing process to take place. Therefore, the relational framework of a HeartPath practitioner is grounded in the science of compassion to facilitate the healing process listening and validating the individual's life story.

Compassion becomes a celebration, not based on feelings of pity, but feelings of togetherness. We can rejoice at another's joy in celebration and grieve at another's sorrow. Both are dimensions that are integral to true compassion. Celebration becomes a path of forgetting ego in order to remember that we are all connected through our kinship. This acknowledgment of kinship is a deeper understanding of why we all come together.

Because words are powerful, and thoughts and beliefs that we carry produce energy around us, the narrative process has a healing process that can move mountains. This is also the reason that we resonate with quotes, poetry, and stories, because they allow us to connect to God's energy. The narrative process helps us to attach meaning to our life stories. It is certain that you can think of many stories that have touched your life, maybe even changed your life. You may also remember testimonies shared by others' trials of life that have given you strength. According to Michael White, "Meanings derived in this process of interpretation are not neutral in their effects on our lives, but have real effects on what we do on the steps that we take in life…we live by stories that we have about our lives." It is in this way we see a path unfold before us. It is in this way we discover our HeartPath. Our personal myths are powerful in that they forcefully shape our beliefs and convictions, thereby providing an active and dynamic influence on the future.

Chapter Seven
HeartPath Healing Techniques

"The best and most beautiful things cannot be seen or touched—they must be felt with the heart."
—Helen Keller

HeartPath practitioners work with people within an individual's belief system. It is not the practitioner's position to try to change the client's personal belief system, but to offer possibilities, to expand an understanding of what they already believe. Meeting your client "where they are" promotes a sense of intimacy and trust that facilitates healing. Conversely, anything that promotes a sense of isolation may lead to chronic stress and, ultimately, to illnesses such as heart disease. Even the word "heal" comes from the Indo-European "to make whole." In Sanskrit, the word "yoga" means "to yoke," to bring together, sometimes translated as "union." These are very old ideas.

Socrates recommended to all his students to "know thyself," wherein our whole being becomes involved.

Students in the helping professions are encouraged to know themselves; "physicians heal thyself." Our spirit within us attempts to understand our whole self in who we really are and why we are here. As a HeartPath practitioner, we must know ourselves so that we can avoid transferences and countertransferences with our client.

The HeartPath practitioner will pay attention to the focus of providing a safe environment for the client that enables truth in sharing to be expressed without fear of being judged, rejected, or given advice. This opens the way to genuine healing and is profoundly transformative. It is transformative in ways that go beyond what we can measure and, ultimately, it is such experiences that are often the most motivating and valuable to people. A safe environment also enables truth to be expressed, which opens the way to real healing and is profoundly transformative.

The HeartPath healing techniques involve the following:

1. Establish a rapport with your client so that trust becomes very clear within the therapeutic relationship. This takes time depending on each individual client and will become evident when the client begins to pronounce his or her trust.

2. Assess the client's belief system relative to his or her understanding of what spirituality means to him or her.

3. Ask the client to remember back as far as he or she can and write down the earliest memory he or she has that had significant meaning attached to it. This is to access his or her heart memory in a real way for him or her.

4. Ask the client to make a list of other life events that he or she believes had a profound effect on him or her. Profound effects would be anything that moved him or her to make decisions in his or her life and reflect upon his or her past, present, and future life.
5. Assist him or her to reflect back by using open-ended questions and asking him or her what he or she believes he or she learned from these life events.
6. Ask the client to draw a line representing his or her life path. Ask him or her if he or she feels like he or she is at a fork in his or her path that will require a decision on which path he or she needs to continue down. This helps him or her look at decision-making and the consequences decisions have on his or her life path.
7. To further explore his or her intrapsychic hopes and dreams, you can utilize various therapeutic techniques that you may already be using in your practice; such as guided imagery, art therapy, narrative (life story), client's personal journals, poetic reflections based on the client's poems, and dream journals. Facilitate guided interpretation of his or her dreams based on what the client feels the dream may be speaking to them.
8. To help keep the client intact with his or her "whole self," you can keep him or her focused on his or her spiritual body, mental state, emotional state, and physical state of being. You can use a simple rating scale of one through ten with one being low and ten being high. This can be

used as a simple ongoing assessment tool for life goals and planning.

9. This is a combination of narrative techniques and the reflection of compassion to the client, as mentioned in chapter six. This healing work brings the client to an awareness of his or her HeartPath giving meaning and purpose to his or her life and his or her past life events, good and bad.
10. All sessions end with a prayer, reading of a poem, story, or saying "narrative" related to his or her session, with meditation of reflection.

As you begin to deal with relational issues, it is important to assess if there are any current unresolved issues from current or past relationships. Ask the client if he or she would like to pray or enter meditation practice through guided imagery or the heart prayer. The emphasis of the heart prayer is to bring his or her focus back to his or her heart for healing. Metaphorically, any past or present hurts would place holes in his or her heart. Through guided imagery, you can ask the client to picture his or her heart and see any holes or dark spots that he or she believes are attached to memories or current painful life relationships. Sometimes it helps the client's "visualization" by asking them to draw a picture of their heart, drawing and coloring in darkened circles of various sizes that represent their painful life events. You can then ask the client to picture God, his or her higher being, an angel, Jesus, white light, or other spiritual symbols for his or her belief system. Ask the client to picture the holes in his or her heart being healed and his or her heart beginning to turn red and glowing with new life and light. Then ask the client to place this new heart back in his or her chest, again specifying that this is done symbolically.

As always, with guided imagery, it is important to bring the client back into his or her presence in the office by using breathing techniques, up to three breaths in and out. Breathing in through his or her nose and exhaling through his or her mouth. Ask him or her how he or she feels and what he or she hopes to do with his or her new heart. Many clients express that they saw the holes in their heart close and do feel better after this exercise. Utilization of soft instrumental music, waterfall sounds, candles, or soft lighting are recommended any time you are using self-hypnosis and guided imagery.

Each session will build upon the previous by helping the client begin to see his or her heart spiritual, heart physical, heart mental, heart emotional within the concept of a "healing journey." As he or she grows in an understanding that he or she is created as a "whole being," he or she will learn to follow a heart-healthy lifestyle for every area of his or her life. The illustration on the following page is a good way to draw out the basic way to begin to see ourselves as a "whole being." Notice that the mind is to the left of the heart, and the emotions are to the right of the heart. The spiritual component is on the top of the picture, and the physical is at the base as the foundation of our grounding in the world. This drawing may be used as an assessment tool for the practitioner and increased awareness for the client. The client is asked to rate each area on a scale from 1–10 with one being low on the scale (not good) up to ten being high (excellent). Practitioner will go over daily life practices that will facilitate improvements in each of these areas.

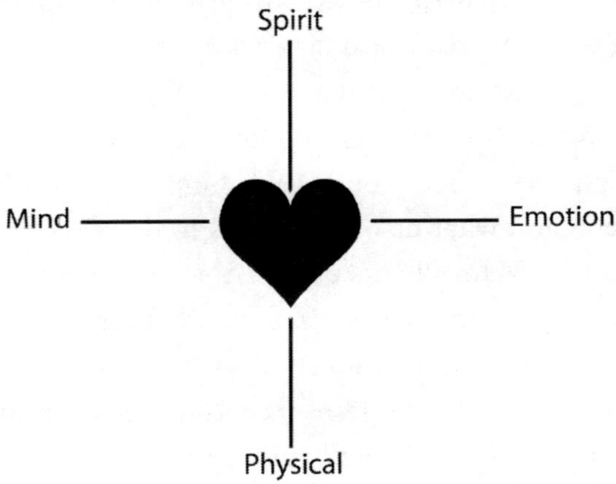

Once your client begins to see the change in the way he or she sees his or her life and feels about his or her personal HeartPath, he or she will begin to connect his or her personal purpose and meaning in his or her life. He or she will also pay close attention to people he or she meets and things that people say that are significant as synchronicity of his or her life. He or she also begins to identify things that are happening to him or her as the formation of his or her path and clearly see why things that have happened all happened for a reason and a purpose. He or she will find new meaning in his or her relationships, which will begin to make sense to him or her.

Drawings: A Narrative Process

> "You read the face of the sky and of the earth, but you have not recognized the one who is before you, and you do not know how to read this moment."
>
> —The Gospel of Thomas

We all remember the phrase "a picture is worth a thousand words." For many people, writing or speaking their life story is not always how they feel they can best express themselves. When working with adults, adolescents, and children, there are powerful revelations that come from drawings as a telling of a person's story. Children express well through drawings, and it is something they enjoy doing. At times, children and adolescents feel that it is easier to write his or her feelings down than to try to talk about them. Drawings may be free drawings or guided. With guided drawings, you can simply draw or place a heart sticker or other symbols in the middle of the paper and see what that brings out in the person's drawing.

> "The heart is the symbol of love when it is right side up. When it is upside down it is the symbol of hate."
>
> Comment by a seven-year-old child

The heart symbol has been celebrated in many ways. Valentine's Day, for example, has created a day to honor loving relationships for adults and children alike. For children in school, this day is a day of magic and mystery, wondering from whom they received a special Valentine's Day card. In a small way, this helps build his or her self-esteem.

This may be the only day that some of the more "unpopular" children are acknowledged in a positive way by peers.

Drawing in journals may also be free-flowing or guided by the practitioner. The drawings provide a portal of telling stories, conveying metaphors, presenting an individual's perspective, and the ability to find meaning. When a problem or anxiety has been externalized by the child or adolescent in a drawing, then it is the perfect time to confront the problem-laden behavior and validate the worth of the creator. Also, when a problem or anxiety has been externalized from a drawing, by the child or adolescent, the corresponding narrative it presents is the opportunity to process in counseling.

The following illustration is an example of a free-flowing drawing based on asking the client to focus on her heart.

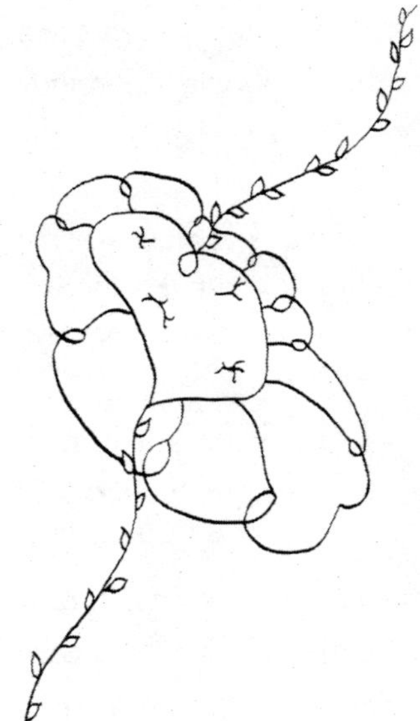

This picture was drawn by a fifteen-year-old girl who described it as a cloud surrounding a heart with cracks because her heart had not been fully healed. The vine was symbolic of connecting the heart to eternity.

The narrative qualities of children's drawings also provide ways of understanding meaning from the child's perspective. Drawings allow the child to present impressions of his or her inner world and responses to the surrounding environment. When working with adolescents and adults, they are amazed at times as to what they end up drawing in expressing how they see his or her life path. The phenomenon is the heart-mind connection, which is expressed from the creative and inspirational spirit within all of us.

Self-Analysis

> "My life is a story of the self-realization of the unconscious."
>
> —Carl Gustav Jung, 1875–1961

To know thyself is not always an easy task in the world we live in today. The more civilized and technical the world has become, the more unconscious and complicated humans have become. This makes it harder to follow our instincts and to sense our intuition in relationship to our divine source, self, and others. In the current growing-complicated living conditions, especially in larger cities, the prevalent influence of this busy environment is so strong that it drowns out the still, quiet voice within. Nature is also silenced as more roads are built, and all we see are a few strands of grass or weeds trying to grow up between the cracks in the cement on the sidewalk. The very gift of life that God created to surround us and give us all we need is being swallowed up in mankind's inventions and material creations to make life more convenient.

The world within that encompasses our unconscious inner life reflects the integrative qualities between our heart and spiritual self, i.e., who we really are as children of light. Many of your clients will express dreams that they have and may seek the meaning of the dream.

The world of dreams, visions, and spiritual experiences all attempt to shed light on the light we carry within. Carl Jung stated, "Man does not strive for wholeness; he already has it, he is born with it." Part of knowing ourselves involves the understanding that we have never been separate from our divine source. The Bible tells us that we are created in his image, God's image, so if this is true, and we have faith and believe this, then we are interconnected to all of creation and born in his image as children of light.

> "Ripe are the consistent in heart; they shall see Sacred Unity everywhere."
>
> Matthew 5:8 (KJV) Aramaic Translation

The HeartPath is about connecting our heart to the heart of the God to know and who we really are. When we remember who we are as innocent children, unencumbered by the external world, we find peace and healing. This is why Jesus said to come as little children in order to find the kingdom of God. Pure childlike faith is the main proven ingredient when looking at recorded miracles in healing.

Titus 2:10–12 says, "Not purloining, but shewing all good fidelity; that they may adorn the doctrine of God our Savior in all things. For the grace of God that bringeth salvation hath appeared to all men, Teaching us that, denying ungodliness and worldly lusts, we should live soberly, righteously, and godly, in this present world." By the grace of God he appears to "all men" to reveal no separation, no judgment, and an understanding that the love of God is what draws hurting people to trust in the healing journey. This principal helps us to reflect on the many different paths that all of us take, which all ultimately lead to the same place, back to the heart of God.

The Human Soul

> "For behold the Word, which is the Wisdom of God, is in thy heart as a Light unto thy feet and lantern unto thy paths. It is there as a speaking Word of God in thy soul; and as soon as thou art ready to hear, this eternal speaking Word will speak Wisdom and Love in thy inward parts and bring forth the birth of Christ, with all his holy nature, spirit and tempers, within thee. Hence it was that so many eminent spirits, partakers of the Divine Life have appeared in so many parts of the heathen world; glorious names, as lights hung out by God . . . These were the apostles of a Christ within.
>
> —William Law, 1686–1761

The key to understanding life problems is to remember that we are not the problem. The HeartPath practitioner will process the problem as the problem in order to keep the client from cycling in the victim thought process. When we become victims, it separates us from who we really are, and healing cannot prevail. Reflection on the soul and who we really are should remind us that there is a higher being/divine source/God/guardian angel by our side, supporting us, loving us, and fully aware of where we are and the challenges we face.

There is a dissociation of personality into "outer" and "inner," into "mask" and "soul." Our soul is complex, but can best be described as a personality. This becomes a battlefield of our spirit and mind. The key to the layers of our persona is the mask that one wears to adapt and present to the outer world based on the demands of society, while the inner world or individual self becomes lost and feels separated. Identity with the persona then automatically leads to an unconscious identity with the anima, because when the ego is not differentiated from the persona, it can have no conscious relation to the unconscious processes.

The soul image is produced by our unconscious and conscious energy that is reflective of both our inner and outer attitudes toward life in general. Sometimes these images are of quite unknown or mythological figures. When we have the ability to slow down and reflect upon our life story, we can reconcile events to understand the reason they happened. The focus becomes based on others' opinions, beliefs, theories, and collective tendencies and appears in our outward life while we forget who we really are. Who we really are should illuminate our paths and the realization that there is a love that surrounds the heart of the human soul.

The teachings of the Dead Sea Scrolls and the New Testament actively prepare the believer, in a meditative sense, to enter into divine dialogue and, in a paraphysical way, experience what the Torah says: "And the Lord God formed man of the dust of the ground, and breathed into his nostrils the breath of life; and man became a living soul" (Genesis 2:7). The word soul, or *nephesh*, comes from the root word in Hebrew, *nafash*, which means to rest. Psalm 42:1–3 shares an intimate divine dialogue with God, "As the hart panteth after the water brooks, so panteth my soul after thee, O God. My soul thirsteth for God, for the living God: when shall I come and appear before God? My tears have been my meat day and night, while they continually say unto me, Where is thy God?"

Do you ever wonder why people come into your life? Each one seems to bring another piece of the puzzle, just as you are a piece of this grand puzzle called life. Understanding the essence of synchronicity is an important part of acknowledging the HeartPath. The whole is made up of the existence and being, the manifested and the unmanifested, the world and God. Become aligned with the whole, become a conscious part of the interconnectedness of the whole and its purpose. When we honor our life and the people who come along our path, our eyes are opened to not only who we are but what our purpose is.

This is a quote from a poem written several years ago called "Life's Hermit" about the awakening of the hermit:

The child took the hermit's hand,
Leading him out of the dark cave.
A new world came into view,
everything held light,
it glowed throughout the land.
The answer is simple,
give everything you have
to receive everything you need,
for therein lies,
the Spirit of Truth.

—By Cinthia McFeature

The HeartPath practitioner understands this deeper connectedness that our mind cannot understand. As a vessel for healing, the HeartPath practitioner honors those who come seeking counsel and healing. The poem below reminds us all of those fleeting moments that are so critical to be acknowledged along our life path.

"Fleeting Moments"

Precious moments,
seem closer together,
each moment more fleeting
than the last.
Long made plans seem to change;
as the moon is full once again.
Life can twist and mold us
into emotions we cannot grasp,
human love is not always enough,
when the one you are with,
draws you away from yourself,

till you have lost your way home.
Ah, but all those memories,
keep pictures in our minds,
knowing we can't go back,
yesterday is only in our hearts,
also present with eternity.
Experiences make life rich,
like a synchronistic symphony,
teaching us to give back to those
who come into our path,
the HeartPath,
reflecting everything we have learned,
and all truth manifested in love.

—By Cinthia McFeature

Healing Journey: HeartPath

As mentioned in the earlier chapters, our life stories are what formulate our path, our journey, our awakening to real love. The healing journey has always been with us and is always present. We simply need to pay close attention to our life experiences by honoring the people who come into our lives. We may also be amazed by the simple, yet deep words of wisdom that come out of the "mouths of babes." God reveals his presence omnipotent and omniscient, opening our spiritual eyes to see our life purpose, and gives our lives meaning. Nothing you will ever do is as important as discovering the meaning of your life.

We find meaning in our life when we connect to our passions, found within the desires of our heart:

1. We participate in our own reality—we are cocreators.
2. Pay attention to others who are a part of our reality.
3. Watch for underlying agendas of others that may not align with your passion and goals.
4. Make an effort to surround yourself with coparticipants that help you learn and grow along your life path.
5. Honor others' belief systems as a possibility, even if you don't agree with what that person believes. Operate out of love and not judgment.
6. Look at each day as an opportunity to have an impact in someone's life. We may be unaware of entertaining angels and the impact may be eternal.

Choosing to live life in a mindful state means paying close attention to everything you see, hear, smell, touch, and feel. Children have a way of keeping us in a mindful state as they point out the little things that we are too busy to notice. When we truly listen to the "still quiet voice" inside that speaks to us, we will find that there is always guidance available. The challenge of life is to learn how to recognize and heed them. We are interwoven, and we can learn from one another's journey.

The inner spiritual journey is critical because it opens a path to a universal pattern. Because we understand that our meaning gives us purpose, it is important that we take our place among those who have answered the call of the

Creator to come and complete creation. It is our destiny as we seek the true heart of God.

Initiation of Heart Prayer Meditation Power of Prayer

> I beseech thee for to draw us up ... to the height of thy dark inspired speakings where all things of divinity be covered and hid under the sovereign-shining darkness of wisest silence.
>
> —Part of the Prayer attributed to St. Denis, circa 13th century

The power of prayer is something that has been proven to work throughout the history of mankind. It is a force that cannot be spoken or transmitted as the written word. The feelings and intentions that are reflected from the words of the prayer are part of the focus of the HeartPath. The heart is the feeling center. It is the feeling of our prayers that opens the door and illuminates our paths to the force of the seen as well as the unseen (Braden, 2000). Research has shown that the feeling behind the prayer—the faith behind the prayer—is the key factor to the prayer. The feeling is the prayer; God knows our hearts. Our words are in essence a code designed to create the feeling and a belief, and the feeling is the power of the prayer.

Open Heart Prayer

Praying preparation: The best way to pray is from a pure heart. Take the following steps to be more within your heart. Close your eyes, begin deep breathing, in through your nose and out through your mouth, relax each part of your body so that your brain is not dominating, ask your brain to smile to your heart and your heart to smile back to your brain to establish harmony. Smiling not only changes a facial expression, but can also make the brain produce endorphins, which reduce physical and emotional pain and give a greater sense of well-being. Touch your heart (the center of your chest) with one or three fingers to stimulate your heart with focused attention. Begin to pray with your feeling and deep intention. Note: This does not have to be a specific memorized or recited prayer. The practitioner can lead the prayer by reading a prayer or scripture that connects to the client's belief system. The following prayer is an example of an open-heart prayer.

> Divine Source, we thank You for all the blessings we have been receiving.
>
> Divine Source, please bless our hearts so that all anger and related negative energy be replaced with Your Love and Light.
>
> Divine Source, bless our hearts so that all arrogance and related negative energy be replaced with Your Love and Light.
>
> Divine Source, bless our hearts so that all jealousy, envy and related negative energy are replaced with Your Love and Light.
>
> Divine Source, bless our hearts so that all greediness, cunningness and related negative energy are replaced with Your Love and Light.
>
> Divine Source, bless our hearts so that we realize that we have to forgive each other to be

closer to You. Bless us to be able to forgive sincerely all the people who have done wrong to us. (Realize all the people who have done wrong to you, even if they are still hurting you, and forgive them one by one, sincerely.)

Divine Source, bless us so that we realize that Your Love always forgives. Bless us to be able to realize all of our mistakes to You and others, to regret and ask for forgiveness for all of our mistakes wholeheartedly. (Be aware of all the mistakes you have made, one by one, regret them and ask for forgiveness.)

Divine Source, forgive us all of our mistakes, done purposefully or not. Bless our hearts so that all fears, worries and burdens caused by our mistakes, and related negative energy be replaced with Your Love and Light.

Divine Source, bless our hearts so that all negativities and impurities that have kept us away from You all this time, together with their seeds and roots, be removed from our hearts and ourselves, and pushed away to wherever they are supposed to be and be replaced with Your Love and Light.

Divine Source, bless us so that Your Love and Light fill our hearts, strengthen our hearts, feeling, compassion and longing for You so that we can feel, enjoy and appreciate Your Love. Let our whole heart and whole self be filled with calmness, peace, happiness and Your Love all the time.

Divine Source, bless, guide and help us so that all of our thoughts, words and actions are always in accordance with Your Love and Light.

Divine Source, bless us so that we can become Your instrument in distributing Your Love and

Light to others unconditionally.

Divine Source, may all beings love you completely and continuously.

Divine Source, please accept our love. (Offer your love to Divine Source with all your heart, soul and mind.)

Divine Source, let Your Love and Light radiate without limit, fill, illuminate and purify all beings, the entire Earth, the Universe and all existences.

Divine Source, let Your Kingdom be real and only things that are in accordance with Your Love and Light be the Consciousness that may happen in all existences.

Thank you, Divine Source.

Amen.

—Retrieved from
www.padmacahaya.com, 2007

Another prayer that can be used with guided imagery, and the prayer that this practitioner utilized with this case study, is as follows:

Jesus Heart Healing Prayer

1. Ask the client to get comfortable, begin to relax, and close his or her eyes.

2. Ask the client to breath in and out deeply three times (symbolic of the Father, Son, and Holy Spirit). Breath in through the nose and exhale through the mouth.

3. Ask the client to picture walking in a forest, down the beach, or in a place that he or she likes to go to be alone.

4. Tell the client that he or she will see someone walking toward them in a white robe, and he has light coming from his eyes and a smile on his face. It appears to be Jesus, and he is asking for your heart.
5. Tell the client to hold his or her heart symbolically in his or her hands and hold it before Jesus. Tell the client that he or she will see dark holes in his or her heart, which represent hurt and pain. You may ask your client to respond when he or she sees the holes and ask how many holes there are.
6. Tell the client that Jesus is taking his forefinger and touching each of the holes in his or her heart and that the holes are closing up one by one as Jesus touches the holes, and there is light coming from his fingertip.
7. Tell the client to symbolically place his or her "new heart" back into his or her chest.
8. Tell the client to look at Jesus and give thanks. You will want to end in a simple prayer of giving thanks to Jesus for healing the client's heart.
9. Tell the client to take another three deep breaths and open his or her eyes slowly.

After conducting this prayer with the guided imagery, Mary, in the single case study, following in Chapter Eight, reported that she felt that she did have a new heart that had been healed by Jesus. She stated that she did see Jesus during the heart prayer and that she felt calm and at peace.

Healing a Broken Heart

HeartPath healing is the process by which the individual will work on transmuting anger into peace, fear into joy, sorrow into happiness, rejection into acceptance, resentment into forgiveness, hatred into love, and apathy into unconditional love. It is a process of coming to the awareness of the existence of destructive emotions and learning how to work through them and into our consciousness and express them with love. It is a process of healing ourselves from emotional trauma of all types, regardless of origin or duration in our life. The HeartPath is intended to help the individual uncover and overcome emotional trauma.

Acceptance is the key to all healing. Learning to accept ourselves and love ourselves is the path to forgiveness and divine heart healing. Self-analysis is the first step in this process, which can be done in mediation, deep concentration, contemplation, or journal writing. The process involves bringing up any painful memories one by one and analyzing them. We have to be honest in looking at ourselves and the mistakes we have made. We must come to the point where we can begin to accept ourselves and others in the same way, in order to accept what they did, and that we did the best we could do.

Any form of meditation can be used in this process. Meditation includes healing breathing, relaxation, intentional prayer, or meditation combined with yoga. Deep concentration may enable the individual to work his or her way into a state of deeper contemplation. Contemplation can be done while helping others and therefore helping yourself.

Journaling is a process wherein you write down your thoughts and feelings about a topic and keep writing until you have exhausted the matter. You can pick a single painful incident and write about it until you have reached the point that you are willing to accept you and the other person that may have been involved in the painful incident.

Unconditional love is not possible for most humans. *Agape* is the Greek word for the love of God in a renewed mind into manifestation. We will spend this lifetime trying to love more and more. This practice includes being aware of our thoughts and thinking loving thoughts. Look at situations and say, "I love this." Look at other people and say, "I love you" silently and meaningfully to yourself no matter what. Feel the love for the divine and everything and everybody no matter what. Just love.

> "Love is a voice the heart can understand, the warmth and comfort of another's hand. A precious moment caught, a secret told. A thing of beauty, a thing of Gold."
>
> —Author unknown

Every attitude we have is an expression of our intention to express that attitude. Find the attitude. There is always an intention underlying that attitude. Finally, change our intention and we can change our attitude. Most of us think that we can hide our intentions and attitudes from others. We cannot. Our attitudes, backed by our intentions, express themselves in the way we deal with life. Even our hesitations, facial expressions, gestures, words, and the emotions behind our words can betray our true intentions and attitudes toward others. We read people the same way that they read us.

We can change our minds by making a decision and believing we can. We change our intentions by releasing an old intention and making a new intention. The HeartPath is always focused on intention because it is there in the core of our heart that intentions begin. The secret is that love heals everything. Love is healing. Love is the divine healing energy. Love is the divine. The divine heals all things. According to Saint Francis, and many saints of all religions, the divine is love.

The heart has a way of communicating when we have hurt someone or when someone has hurt us. Over time, the heart begins to harden if a person feels abandoned and finds that he or she is unable to feel empathy, compassion, or love for others. We understand that if the heart does not get blood, then it turns black. Therefore, metaphorically speaking, when a person's heart becomes hardened by bitterness and anger, it turns spiritually dark.

The one who created us understands a broken heart and is present in our suffering. We look within to find a spark of hope, which is part of who we really are. We may lose our way for a short time in the midst of emotional pain, but when we focus on the love of God, we fall into his arms and find true peace and trust.

Hearts are tender simple and pure
With minds of hardened reflection

Ruffled or tossed or unable to endure
The risk of impending rejection.
—John Stringer, "Sweet Circumstance"

A broken heart results from hurtful words and hurts deeply, and unfortunately is a great part of an individual's life story and human suffering. Many times, words form a false perception of who we really are, because we have listened to people who have hurtful agendas, most of the time stemming from his or her own pain. This is what forms unhealthy relationships as they feed off each other's pain and view life as a victim. The words they speak enforce a person's place of fear and victimization.

> "The true harvest of my daily life is somewhat as intangible and indescribable as the tints of the morning or evening. It is a little star dust caught, a segment of the rainbow which I have clutched."
> —Henry David Thoreau

Heart Connection

Striving for a whole heart is equal to healing the whole person through the heart physical impact, heart mental impact, heart emotional impact, and heart spiritual impact. Our hearts speak to us in so many ways. We must listen to our hearts and understand that each area works together to give us breath life with a spiritual connection to our higher being and all of creation.

Consider Proverbs 4:20–23 (NIV) regarding the heart: "My son, pay attention to what I say; listen closely to my words. Do not let them out of your sight, keep them within your heart; for they are life to those who find them and health to a man's whole body. Above all else, guard your heart, for it is the wellspring of life." Jesus recognized the importance of the heart in a person's life. In Mark 7:21–23 he stated, "For from within, out of the heart of men, proceed evil thoughts, adulteries, fornications, murders, thefts, covetousness, wickedness, deceit, lewdness, an evil eye, blasphemy, pride, foolishness. All these evil things come from within and defile a man." It is clear that the heart has a great influence on our overall health, physically, emotionally, mentally, and spiritually. The symbol of the heart is one way of self-examination. The heart as a home connects to our eyes, ears, smell, taste, and touch and with our conscious mind. Metaphorically speaking, the rooms in our heart consist of emotions, heritage, accessible memories, inaccessible memories, feelings, beliefs, desires, and instincts.

It is important to understand a person's belief and value system. We all have different beliefs about our family, our work, our community, and our nation. Much of a person's behavior is based on what he or she believes to be good. Beliefs affect how we think, the way we perceive our world, and, ultimately, how we act. Along with this, it is important to understand a person's heritage, which is also stored in heart memory and is a part of who they are. A person's heritage and upbringing strongly affects how he or she sees and responds to the world around them.

Our desires are what drive our heart for power, wealth, pleasure, or sexual satisfaction. A person may also have the core desire to please others and have the approval from others for self-esteem. There are those who have a creative desire to do something that is unique to an expression of self. We must consider the desire for spiritual knowledge and for knowing the truth and knowing God. Dr. Carl Jung was asked in an interview if he believed in God, and he responded, "No, I know him." This is the difference between a religious person who has the desire to please others, such as to be in Church on Sunday, and those who acknowledge God daily throughout the week. To be true to our heart we must be true to ourselves and true to God.

Heart memory is also stored in our hearts. There are many memories that are lost to our conscious recall. Research has proven that memories of difficulties before birth or trauma during or immediately after birth can have long-lasting effects on mental and physical health. The diagnosis of reactive attachment disorder is an example of the importance of nurturing in the first year of life, even though this is not available in our conscious memory. Heart memory also seems to attach to all of our senses and is strong in the areas where we place meaning in our lives.

A person's instincts, which are deep-seated and almost an automatic response of the mind, refer to fundamental needs in a person's life. Instincts are powerful. We can seldom override them. It is possible to starve oneself to death, but even this requires great mental effort. Techniques such as biofeedback can help reverse thoughts tied to areas that try to override God-given instincts, for example, in working with individual's who may be dealing with eating disorders.

There are interactions that occur between the various

areas of our heart. The events we experience stimulate the emotions and influence the desires and drives. In the same way, what is in the subconscious mind can come into the conscious mind and influence it. Some emotions or desires enter quietly; others may burst violently into the conscious mind and even out through the door of expression to the outside world. In fact, even during our sleep, the subconscious mind remains active, and our dreams are the processing of present and past symbols and events.

The heart also has an inner heart that is in contact with the spiritual world, with God. This place in our heart must be guarded. This place strongly influences our spiritual, psychological, and physical health. This is the place of prayer and meditation and a place of peace when we feel and connect to the heart of God.

Heart Physical Impact

We know that heart disease kills over 710,000 people yearly in the United States; therefore, it is worthy of doing what we can to not become a statistic. The heart is the most important muscle in our body because if it stops working, everything else stops. The heart, on an average, beats one hundred thousand times each day and circulates about two thousand gallons of blood. The heart is the epicenter of your body and is fed with blood from coronary arteries that are responsible for keeping the heart well supplied with a lifeline of oxygenated, nutrient-rich blood.

When the blood supply to the heart becomes severely reduced or cut off because one or more arteries become blocked, a heart attack occurs. Blood clots are formed when arterial plaque filled with cholesterol builds up in the arteries and becomes unstable and inflamed. Within a complex sequence of biochemical events, it then develops a crack or fissure, which releases substances that encourage clot formation. It is usually the clot attached to a plaque that causes a heart attack because no blood can get through to supply oxygen and other nutrients to the working heart muscle.

We need to discuss with our doctor what we can do to keep our heart healthy through diet and exercise and possibly a medication regime, if needed. There are many new heart-screening tests that can help us, along with our primary care physician, keep an eye on our heart health. Some of these are the exercise stress test, coronary calcium scoring CT (CAD), Ultrafast CT, lipoprotein test, cardiac catheterization, and stress echocardiogram. It is important to also understand that our spiritual health, emotional health, and mental health all have an impact on our heart.

Heart Spiritual Impact

Seeking the heart of God is the foundation of the HeartPath. The Doctrine of Ones says that the divine is everything and that everything is the divine. Everything is the great mystery, and the great mystery is everything. Everything is the Great Spirit, and the Great Spirit is everything. Everything is the grand architect of the universe, and the grand architect of the universe is everything. Everything else said about the divine is a personal belief and a personal decision. The universal gnostic viewpoint of all these beliefs and all these decisions are correct for that individual, but may not be correct for others. The HeartPath is a narrow path for one, for each of us to walk in hope and in faith on our own spiritual journey, and at times someone carries us. The healing takes place as we seek God, the divine, and/or the Creator. After all, if we understand that we are one with the divine, who is best to understand us than the divine and one day ourselves?

The HeartPath practitioner understands that we ultimately have to have divine acceptance, forgiveness, and love in order to heal ourselves. We rely on the divine acceptance, forgiveness, and love to help other people heal themselves. We commit to pray, contemplate, and meditate with the divine so that we always have the strength, not by our strength, but by the strength of the divine, to follow our call and purpose.

The HeartPath practitioner seeks the heart of God, the divine, in order to help all who seek counsel. The word heart awakens, first of all, the idea of a material heart, of the vital organ that throbs within our bosom, and which we vaguely realize as intimately connected not only with our own physical body, but also with our emotional and moral life. Now, this heart of flesh is currently accepted as the emblem of the emotion and moral life with which we associate it. The place assigned to the word heart in symbolic language is also the same word to designate those things symbolized by the heart, as stated in the expressions "to open one's heart," "to give one's heart," etc.

It may happen that the symbol becomes divested of its

material, meaning that the sign is overlooked in beholding only the thing signified. Thus, in current language, the word soul no longer suggests the thought of breath, and the word heart brings to mind only the idea of courage and love. But this is perhaps a figure of speech or a metaphor, rather than a symbol. A symbol is a real sign, whereas a metaphor is only a verbal sign; a symbol is a thing that signifies another thing, but a metaphor is a word used to indicate something different from its proper meaning. Finally, in current language, we are constantly passing from the part to the whole, and, by a perfectly natural figure of speech, we use the word heart to designate a person. These ideas will aid us in determining the object of the devotion to the Sacred Heart.

Heart Mental Impact

We know that Jesus used stories and parables to illustrate spiritual things. He gave us guidelines to live our lives by and also showed us with his compassion how to transcend the human mind. Through science and research we have come to an understanding that our bodies are made up of mostly water. We also understand that we have a spiritual body, which is composed of God's energy—the Holy Spirit. Learning to meditate on this energy flow as the flow of blood throughout our bodies helps us to focus on our true self.

When Jesus spoke about his anointed body, he was speaking about his spiritual body. When he spoke of the healing blood he was speaking of the healing spiritual energy and transferring those healing thoughts to the heart where it can be stored in heart memory. Heart memory is powerful because it connects to all of our senses—taste, touch, smell, auditory, sight, as well as spiritual ears to hear and eyes to see. "If a person who was rich enough in this world's goods saw that one of his brothers or sisters was in need, but closed his heart to that person, how could the love of God be living in him?" (1 John 3:17). I personally believe that the mind of Christ is connected to our spirit by the Holy Spirit through an inner sanctuary of our heart that leads us to fulfill Matthew 5:8, which says that the "pure in heart shall see God."

Heart Emotional Impact

We must always be aware of the intensity of the heart's emotional impact of painful life events. Research conducted in 1947 by Dr. Hans Jenny introduced a new science called Cymatics. This research revealed that there were both physiological and psychological effects from the emotions that generated feelings of forgiveness and anger. Cymatics is the relationship between vibration and form. It is a vibratory template that creates pressure in our cells and affects our DNA so that the quality of emotion may define the quality of our DNA. Positive emotions were shown to have a high frequency, which was healthy for our cells, whereas negative emotions had a low frequency, which was not healthy for our body's cells. There was noted immune response depression. Therefore, a person's ability to forgive and reflect compassion toward others had a high frequency based on the connection between thoughts, feelings, and emotions. According to the Dead Sea Scrolls, the power of thought was given to the sons and daughters of men and that man had forgotten the power of thoughts.

An emotion is an internal response to an external event, a strong psychic energy that influences the body as well as the rest of the mind. Science has now shown through quantum physics that emotions have power to change chemicals inside our bodies. These emotions have an effect on our neuropeptides in our mind. This has an influence on other organ activity in our bodies.

Negative emotions such as anger, fear, shame, or envy are kept in the subconscious mind and continue to stimulate the production of neuropeptides that act on blood pressure, digestion, and other organs and systems in the body. Chronic production of these neruopeptides by negative emotions may eventually result in a physical or psychological illness.

Feelings differ from emotions; they are based on the impressions we have about ourselves, the world around us, and the circumstances in which we find ourselves. Depending on how we perceive our circumstances is how we feel happy or sad, comfortable or uncomfortable, and secure or insecure.

Chapter Eight

Application of HeartPath Interventions: A Single Case Study

The authors will attempt to apply the HeartPath principles and interventions to a particular single case study that portrays a depressed female client. The client will be named Mary for the sake of privacy and confidentiality.

An examination of four life domains that represent an individual's life journey reflect his or her physical, emotional, cognitive, and spiritual dimensions of self are utilized for identification and guided reflection throughout the healing process.

> "I have not been able to work because of uncontrollable crying spells. I have also had panic attacks that I cannot control. I understand what they mean when they say that depression hurts. I hurt all over my body."
>
> —Mary, Single Case Study

Single Case Study

Mary reports being diagnosed with fibromalysia, depression, and anxiety symptomatolgy. She also reports having breathing difficulties, manifesting mild-moderate panic episodes, reportedly frequent at times. She reports working in a highly stressful job for the past ten years. She also reports physical decompensation associated with significant exacerbating depression and panic over the last year.

Mary begins the HeartPath healing process: 1) Obtain a medical evaluation by asking Mary how long it has been since she has acquired a physical exam with blood work. If more than a year has passed, she should be encouraged to consult with her physician. Conditions can bring on symptoms of depression and anxiety. Preexisting and coexisting physical conditions can underlie and aggravate presently reported depressive and/or anxiety symptomatology. 2) Telling of her life story. The practitioner will cocreate an analysis of Mary's story, seeking themes and patterns in her responses. The practitioner will then create a narrative, verbal or written, that speak to the experiences of Mary, requiring empathetic understanding. The practitioner remains sensitive to subtle and deep tones of the client's language and conversational dialogue. The practitioner pays special attention to the time and space of the told story in coconstructing Mary's narrative. The practitioner will "be present with Mary" is describing her lived experience in a genuine way and reflects upon the experience that emerges from the dialogue or conversation between the practitioner and Mary. The practitioner-client experience involves mood, emotions, energy, and feelings of relational quality that speak to the deeper understanding of her lived experience.

This process will give insight into how Mary expresses dialogue of her lived experience relevant to the telling of her story. The process allows for assessing the communication and use of right and left-brain domains. Verbalized or written narratives reflect the essence of these words or phrases, which then generate themes and patterns that connect to the narrative. The practitioner will search for interpretation of Mary's narrative, reflecting these connecting themes that are identified through the four life domains—physical, emotional, mental, and spiritual. The practitioner addresses these presented themes identified from Mary's told story.

An inductive process, line-by-line analysis is conducted and transcribed narrative will identify and code units of meaning. These categorized units of meaning are organized into identified central themes relevant to Mary's lived experience. Each sentence is subjected to the question, "What does this sentence reveal about the phenomenon or experience being described?" Each central theme is compared to Mary's unit of meaning (interrelational dimension) to ensure the accuracy of relevant meaning to each central theme. Finally, themes are compared to intrarelational dimensions across the spectrum of reviewing the data.

The practitioner can utilize color-coding to identify the themes that are categorized into the life domains, the physical, mental, emotional, and spiritual. The practitioner is mindful of developing categories rather than simply labeling topic areas.

The practitioner will look for informal patterns or emerging concepts such as repetitive words, metaphors, and reoccurrence of emotional intensity. The interview process with the participant will reflect the conceptual findings by giving examples of written narrative from the transcripts, then summarizing what was learned from Mary's lived experience of multiple losses of relationships throughout her life and evaluating the lived experience of Mary.

During this process, an intrapsychic flow of memory and experiences manifest, revealing the structure of lived experience and allowing an illumination to process self issues through identification and evaluation of the client's generated themes and patterns in order to make sense of her lived experiences associated with physical and emotional difficulties, such as fibromalysia and depression or anxiety.

Life Domains

The practitioner refers back to the client's reported life journey expressed through his or her "told story" relevant to "who they are." The practitioner captures the client's lived experience through reflection and illumination relevant to his or her verbal and/or written narrative. These recollected memories and experiences allow a healing transformational journey to occur that presents with mobility and movement versus stagnation in life. The practitioner can utilize various "portholes" or windows, so to speak, to manifest these transformations such as audio taping, drawings, and journaling. These transformed experiences form the client's generated narrative/themes and patterns of meaning, allowing the client to experience a healing journey. The four life domains are as follows:

Physical domain refers to the physical body and everything that is defined by the client as a physical problem or barrier to his or her quality of life. In our physical body or bodily presence, we both reveal something about ourselves and we always conceal something at the same time, not necessarily consciously or deliberately, but rather in spite of ourselves. When the body is the object of someone else's gaze, it may lose it naturalness, or instead, it may happen that it grows enhanced in its modality of being.

Mental domain refers to the psychological factors that pertain to the way the client processes thoughts. The HeartPath practitioner is looking at various mental health disorders that may have caused significant depression, anxiety, or mood disorders.

Emotional domain is the emotional pain or elation that results from the client's family history and environmental factors that are reported in the reported life story. The emotions result in feelings or intentions that have the power to result in healing with coping or destruction with ruminating thoughts leading to hopelessness.

Spiritual domain is the lived relation we maintain with others in the interpersonal space that we share with them. As we meet the other, we are able to develop a conversational relation that allows us to transcend ourselves to the belief in a higher being. Human beings have all searched in this domain of the other, the communal, the social for a sense of purpose in life, meaningfulness, grounds for living, as in the religious experience of meeting God.

The objectivity of utilizing the structured domains is to capture the lived experience of the client reflected in the narrative itself. This brings about a metaphorical and symbolic form to a client's conversational dialogue. The practitioner is acquainted with the four life domains. The practitioner should also pay attention to nonverbal language on what is not being said (silence). Speech rises out of silence, which becomes categorical text or narrative. A strong emphasis is placed in the client's telling of the story, reflecting a rich, in-depth and quality narrative utilized in reaching the goal of transformational healing, the personal and life transformation within the client's healing journey.

Every client should be given the opportunity to tell his or her own story. This is the first step in the healing process through HeartPath healing narrative techniques. Most of us can probably remember numerous times when simply having someone to listen attentively to our struggles seemed to help, even if the listener offered no specific feedback or guidance in the matter. Clients likewise can benefit immensely from having someone with whom to share his or her story. In James 5:16 it reads, "Confess your sins to one another and pray for one another so that you may be healed." In Psalms, David demonstrates how the sharing of his sorrows, fears, and even frustrations, helps him to move through these painful experiences, leading to greater insights and a general receptivity to God. While we understand that simply allowing clients to share his or her pain from his or her stories will not result in resolution to all problems, it nevertheless helps to begin the healing process. During this time, the practitioner also begins to build trust and rapport in order to explore the client's feelings, thoughts, and behaviors, to get a clearer understanding of the problems and issues at hand (Sphar & Smith, 2001).

Initial Intake Transcript

The transcript below is an example of the "telling of the story," utilizing thematic analysis that will generate the common and unique themes from the individual's told life narrative.

Single Case Study–Mary (age 40)

Mary reports multiple relationship losses. She was asked, "Tell me about your life and the relationships you believe have played a role in where you are in your life now. Also, tell me how these life events made you feel and how you feel now."

> I have three children, child one (girl) age 5, child two (girl) age 8, and child three (boy) age 13. We have several pets at our house including three cats, three dogs, and two rabbits. I have been married three times. My first husband I was married to for five years. My second husband I was married to for five years. My third husband I have been married to for three years, and I have been separated for one year. My parents divorced when I was in high school. My mom remarried and was married for ten years. I also have a sister who is five years older than me and lives near me; however, I don't ever see her. She has never been there for me or my mom.

My mom's second husband died a month ago. He was a very good stepfather. My mom was also very close to him up until he passed away. I was always my daddy's girl, and I went fishing with him, worked on home improvement projects with him, and that made my mom mad because she did not want me to have a relationship with my dad. My mom is a very proud person, and she has told me that I was an accident. I still love my mom and accept her for who she is. My mom did not want to see my dad when he was dying. I would not let my father die alone, so I went to him and stayed with him until he died. I was there when my father took his last breath. He was breathing hard, and then he just went to sleep. I lost a part of me when he died. I just feel like I have lost my best friend. My son was five years old when my father died.

My mom spends time with my sister and not me. My children are therefore not close to their grandmother. My husband, whom I have been separated from for one year, has been paying child support. My son does not want to see his dad. He does not have a relationship with his dad. He has never been able to do anything to please his dad. His dad was never home, except for on the weekends, and then he did not want the kids to bother him. He never wants to put forth the effort to see his kids. I don't know what happened because we never argued. He told me that he wasn't happy anymore, and then he moved in with a girlfriend.

I have not been able to work because of uncontrollable crying spells. I have also had panic attacks that I cannot control. I understand what they mean when they say that depression hurts. I hurt all over my body. I have been working for the past seven years. At this time I have high blood pressure, I am a diabetic, and have fibromyalsia, and my depression and anxiety levels are high, resulting in the need for medications. If it were not for my faith in God, I would not have made it this far. At this point in my life I feel very alone. I have no one to turn to because my family is not there for me. I am trying to be strong for my children's sake. I fear I will never meet anyone who could love me and my children. I have never been to counseling, but I realized that I needed help.

Identified Themes–Core and Unique

Depicted Themes	Narrative Text
Spiritual Connection to God	If it were not for my faith in God I would not have made it this far.
Exposure to Partner's Infidelity	He told me that he wasn't happy anymore, and then he moved in with a girlfriend.
Seeking Therapeutic Help (Counseling)	I have never been to counseling, but I realized that I needed help.

Lack of Immediate Family Support	I also have a sister who is five years older than me and lives near me: however, I don't ever see her. She has never been there for me or my mom.
	My son does not want to see his dad. He does not have a relationship with his dad. He has never been able to do anything to please his dad. His dad was never home except for on the weekends and then he did not want the kids to bother him. He never wants to put forth the effort to see his kids.
	I have no one to turn to because my family is not there for me.
Loneliness	At this point in my life I feel very alone.
Reported Depression and Anxiety Symptomatology	I have not been able to work because of uncontrollable crying spells. I have also had panic attacks that I cannot control. I understand what they mean when they say that depression hurts. I hurt all over my body.
Grief	I lost a part of me when he died.
Living for Children	I am trying to be strong for my children's sake.

<table>
<tr><td>Unsure Feelings about the Future</td><td>I fear I will never meet anyone who could love me and my children.</td></tr>
<tr><td>Forgiveness</td><td>My mom is a very proud person, and she has told me that I was an accident. I still love my mom and accept her for who she is.</td></tr>
<tr><td rowspan="2">Multiple Marriages</td><td>I was married three times. My first husband I was married to for five years. My second husband I have been married to for five years. My third husband I have been married to for three years, and I have been separated for one year.</td></tr>
<tr><td>My parents divorced when I was in High School. My mom remarried and was married for ten years.</td></tr>
<tr><td>Physical Health Problems</td><td>At this time I have high blood pressure, I am a diabetic, and have fibromyalsia.</td></tr>
<tr><td>Presence of Pets</td><td>We have several pets at our house including three cats, three dogs, and two rabbits.</td></tr>
</table>

The above depicted themes are only some of the depicted themes that were present in Mary's narrative. Throughout the intake, she was very tearful but understood that telling her story would be a painful process for her. She was told at the end of the intake that she was very strong and that I knew that this must have been very difficult to talk about. I told her that I would like for her to commit to at least four sessions over the next four weeks. She agreed that this healing process by a spiritual health coach/counselor would be helpful.

Once you have discussed with the client the identified themes, you can begin to explore the core issues that have defined reported depression or anxiety symptomatology. With each session, the HeartPath practitioner evaluates each of the areas of the client's overall life, spiritual well-being, physical well-being, mental well-being, and emotional well-being. When the client has an awareness of the importance of this balance, he or she will begin to think in this manner and remember to address each of these areas in his or her life. When the client has been given the opportunity to tell his or her story and reflect on the impact lived experiences have had on his or her lives, the healing process begins. Each healing session concludes with a prayer and/or the option to use the heart prayer or a reading of a poem or story that reflects hope and peace. The choice of how to conclude each session depends on the tone of the session and the individual's belief system. The following identified themes are reflective of Mary's reported narrative.

Fear

> "I fear I will never meet anyone who could love me and my children."
>
> —Quote from Mary, Single Case Study

Fear is a common theme and is a figment of our mind. It is merely a relay of energies that exists in our left brain, for the right brain knows no fear. The heart reacts strongly to fear with fight or flight based on the increase in stress hormones, such as cortisol and epinephrine. At times, fear is a gift because it takes us out of harm's way; however, fear, when taken out of context, can cause our decision-making to become cloudy and confused. Fear can paralyze a person and cause withdrawal. Fear through threats may also be used as a way to control an individual in a relationship. The HeartPath practitioner, working from a place of compassion, does not belittle the client's fear but works within his or her narrative to show him or her that it is a thought that can be overcome. Psalm 27: "The Lord is my light and my salvation; whom shall I fear? The Lord is the strength of my life; of whom shall I be afraid?"

Anger

> "He never wants to put forth the effort to see his kids."
>
> —Quote from Mary, Single Case Study

Recent studies have shown that symptoms of coronary disease occurred much more often among men who were measured as hostile on a personality test compared with others with more conventional risk factors. Anger, like fear, sends a message to the body to prepare for action. The heartbeat quickens and stress hormones are released. However, unlike fear, an angry person may carry these reactions in a chronic state of mind. Should this core theme arise, the HeartPath practitioner will work through the process of surrender, forgiveness, and love in order to release anger, so that it does not have significant impact on the client's physical body. The HeartPath practitioner will also explore the deeper emotional pain through his or her client's narrative to quench the core cause of the anger.

Loss

> "I would not let my father die alone, so I went to him and stayed with him until he died. I was there when my father took his last breath. He was breathing hard, and then he just went to sleep. I lost a part of me when he died. I just feel like I have lost my best friend."
>
> —Quote from Mary, Single Case Study

As a counselor, I have been honored to share my testimony with my clients who have lost a loved one. I was his only daughter, and when my father passed away, I was not able to be with him. I was residing in Tennessee, and my family lived in Salt Lake City, Utah, at that time. I only know that when I was on the plane flying home that his spirit spoke to mine in a "still quiet voice." I heard the words, "I will not be there when you get there, but I am fine now." When I got off the plane, it was no surprise that he was already gone. I asked about the time of his passing, and it was the exact time that his spirit spoke to me.

Like all of us who have lost a loved one, I had to come to a place in my life where I could reconcile this emotion with my thoughts to release it and not allow it to destroy me. I do know that our hearts, through the spirit, are knitted together, and that my father's spirit did speak to me. Sometimes it is hard to see things in the spirit and not give credit to these experiences that are very real. This life event, for me, further validated my belief in eternal life. The story is endless, because we do have eternal life, and my father's story still touches my life and the lives of those he knew and loved.

For those who are left behind, the power of a testimony may provide comfort. I have shared this story many times to offer hope to others seeing his or her loved one again, one day in heaven. I have spoken with many pastors who have told stories of being by the bedside of someone who is dying. They have shared stories that the person, in their final moments, reports seeing family members who have gone before them in their room, waiting to take them home.

According to Rabbi David Wolpe, author of *Making Loss Matter*, in the biblical creation story, God ultimately pronounces the world "good." This world is to therefore be embraced, ingested, greedily explored for the wonders God has given. The variety and depth of the offerings given to us in this world are designed to expand and deepen our souls. We must rope ourselves to the world's wonders and feel its losses, for, ultimately, our end in this world is to grow in soul and spirit. The soul grows through pain as well as joy. Out of pain comes the steepest growth because the resources of the soul are most severely taxed. We grow spiritual muscle by understanding that avoiding pain is sidestepping growth.

When dealing with the loss of a loved one through death, divorce, or family members becoming estranged, there is much pain and grieving. When we try to avoid pain, we narrow our lives. In the end, we are not spared because increasingly, things in the world are seen as occasions for suffering instead of opportunities to grow. The roots of the heart in love are bound up with knowledge of pain and a consciousness of loss. In the end, such love connects us to God. A sense of intimacy returns us with a renewed sense of oneness. The HeartPath then connects the aura of eternity that envelops a love that is encircled in passion of faith and a compassion for life and others that bring true meaning and purpose.

The single case study of Mary, as explored in this book, has demonstrated an individual who presented a unique story of her lived experience presenting themes that reflected both hurt and survival. Her survival appeared to be in the area of her spiritual connection to God. This may also be reflective of our ongoing journeys, which have memories of suffering, especially the deep suffering that comes from the passing of a loved one.

> "To live within the hearts of others is to never die."
> —Author unknown

Loneliness

> "At this point in my life I feel very alone."
> —Quote from Mary, Single Case Study

Dean Ornish (1993) stated that he had a chance to spend a lot of time with the same group of patients over a period of many years who all came to know each other very well. The patients were about as different from each other as you could imagine in age, race, religion, socio-economics, demographics, sex, sexual preference, disease severity; you name it. At first, it seemed the only thing they had in common was heart disease. But over time, he began to realize that many of them had something else in common: an emotional or spiritual heart disease—the same sense of loneliness, isolation, and alienation that I think is epidemic in our culture.

One hundred years ago, people had social networks; they had extended families; they had a church or synagogue that they went to regularly; they had a neighborhood that they grew up in, and they knew all the neighbors; they had a job that they worked at for many years. These days, many people don't have such a sense of community and belonging. Even the nuclear family has melted down. The two-parent family, with children from the same two parents, is the minority now in many parts of this country.

Ornish believes that we are paying a high price for these changes. Part of that price is chronic stress, rooted in widespread feelings of isolation. Many patients I work with tell me, "I feel isolated and alone. I must be lacking something or I wouldn't feel this way, so if only I had more (fill in the blank: money, power, accomplishment, love) then I would be okay, then people would love and respect me, then I wouldn't feel so lonely and isolated."

Once an individual sets up the "if only I had" view of the world, it turns out he or she is likely to feel more stressed. There's a lot at stake because it's not just winning and losing; it's being a winner or a loser that's on the line. He or she believes that losers will be shunned and isolated, whereas everybody loves a winner. Winning and competition (at whatever fills the blank) holds out an illusion of intimacy. Later, he or she finds out life doesn't work that way. "The more you get, the less there is for me." "You only live once, so get it while you can." Even if he or she gets it, it's satisfying only for a little while. It reinforces his or her belief that his or her sense of peace and well-being comes from outside him or herself, and that is what's so seductive.

> Be able to be alone. Lose not the advantage of solitude ... but delight to be alone and single with Omnipresency ... Life is a pure flame, and we live by an invisible sun within us.
>
> —Sir Thomas Browne, 1605–1682

Role of Forgiveness

> "My mom is a very proud person, and she has told me that I was an accident."
>
> —Quote from Mary, Single Case Study

Forgiveness will become easy once you have come to acceptance. When we accept ourselves as a living, breathing spark of the divine, we forgive ourselves. When we come to accept another person, believing that the person was doing the best that he or she could do under the circumstances, it becomes easy to forgive him or her.

Max Lucado stated:

> We have not been sprinkled with forgiveness and now have not been spattered with grace. We have not been dusted with kindness. We have not been immersed in it. We are however, submerged in mercy. We are a minnow in the ocean of his mercy. Let this change us. See if God's love doesn't do for you what it did for the woman in Samaria.

Ephesians 4:32 reads, "And be ye kind to another, tender-hearted, forgiving one another, even as God for Christ's sake hath forgiven you." Also, in Matthew 18:21–22 it reads, "Then came Peter to him, 'Lord how oft shall my brother sin against me, and I forgive him? till seven times?' Jesus saith unto him, 'I say unto thee, Until seven times: but, Until seventy times seven.'" Forgiveness leads to reconciliation between individuals; it involves the reestablishment of a caring relationship in which mutually trustworthy behaviors and thoughts replace untrustworthy behaviors and attitudes.

So as we consider the heart emotional impact, which includes anger, worry, fear, hate, sadness, love, joy, and compassion, we always go back to our belief system that underlies our intentions, which underlies our attitudes and our thoughts. Again, these thoughts will become actions, good or bad. When we lack forgiveness for others who have hurt us, the root of bitterness, anger, worry, fear, and hate will continue to strangle our hearts. Further, when we do not forgive ourselves, we drown in a sea of guilt and sorrow. God has given us the path to forgive by his strength and not by ours alone.

Forgiveness is the window to reconciliation. It allows us to reconcile things that have happened in our lives that have caused us great pain. It allows us to see painful life experiences as a chance to grow spiritually. The reconciliation is not always with the person who caused us pain, but may be just between God and ourselves.

Forgiveness is primarily for creating your peace of mind. It is also to create healing in your life and returns you to a state in which you can live and be capable again of love and trust. Forgiveness may not always lead to reconciliation. Many people forgive an abusive parent but sever contact with that parent. Another example is married couples who reconcile after an affair but do not forgive. It can also be helpful to remember we can change our minds, and a decision to sever contact in the present is often revisited in the future.

Forgiveness is the experience of finding a peace within and can neither be compelled nor stopped by another. Forgiveness and justice are also not the same. You can seek justice with an open heart just as well as with a bitter one.

Painful events can be life-enhancing experiences when we grieve and learn from them. It is important that people remember he or she is a part of all common humanity and focus on what they have done to learn from life experiences. The HeartPath practitioner must not set up expectations of total forgiveness as a feeling, but explain to the client that the act of forgiveness is a spiritual act and may not always be felt with feelings. What a person can do is to make peace with his or her past. He or she can regain his or her ability to trust and love and not blame other people for his or her emotional distress. He or she can be free of the victim role and move forward to a new life. He or she can take more time to count his or her blessings and less time to complain and to reach out and help others. He or she can understand that he or she needs to look more at who he or she becomes and less on what has happened grasp that each day is a fresh start. God's mercies are new every day.

The commonality that threads Mary's story was quite evident in regards to: a) her life prior to a traumatic event; b) during the traumatic event; and c) after the traumatic event. The preconceived assumptions or ideas as discussed in the literature suggests that exposure to traumatic events or experiences are associated with biological, psychological, and social factors. In the single case study of Mary, she was allowed to share her life story relevant to the details of her experiences and, in turn, began to grasp an understanding of her lived experience.

During the remaining sessions, for purposes of this study, Mary was asked on a scale of 1–10 to assess her strengths as she has stood up against the problem. Each area is examined based on the number, which appears from 1–10 for these areas: spiritual, mental, emotional, and physical. This participant/client expressed that she was in the negative numbers for each area. Her results were as follows: Spiritual was a negative 9; mental was a negative 1; emotional was a negative 20; and physical was a negative 1. When viewing the problems from this perspective, it is easier for the person to observe, break down, and identify the effects of the problems. Mary can also articulate how the problems have effected what she thinks of herself as a person, her understanding of self in important social roles, her hopes and dreams, her thoughts, her moods, and even her physical health. She was excited to share her new numbers when she found healing and reported that each area of her life was improving. This gives the client a feeling of control and investment in his or her overall health.

Epilogue

The HeartPath practitioner takes in to consideration the whole person that God has created, looking at the importance of a healthy physical heart, the connection of the heart with our emotions, mind, and most important, spiritual being connected to God. The theoretical framework is a psychospiritual narrative-based practice that reaches out to children, adolescents, and adults who find healing through a heart journey by reconnecting to who they really are in his image. Seeing life through God's eyes, we find true meaning and empowerment for a new life with hope. Narrative approaches are utilized to develop the HeartPath and is the foundational premise that human beings are meaning makers. Through our lived experiences, we make sense out of our world and reconcile life events to ourselves in order to find purpose and direction.

Researchers at the Institute of HeartMath have recently discovered that the heart has more than forty thousand neurons, or brain cells, in heart tissue, revealing that the heart may have intuitive ability. The heart's code is recorded and remembered in every cell in the body as an informational template of the soul. The heart constantly speaks to us within and connects with other's hearts through discernment. Is it then possible that what we have searched for outside ourselves, in trying to connect to the spiritual universe, God, divine source, or higher being, is simply within our hearts? According to Luke 17:21, "The kingdom of God is within."

The HeartPath practitioner must come along side his or her client to facilitate a newfound awareness of "God's presence" based on the "telling of his or her story." The told story becomes a tool for the HeartPath practitioner for exploration and initiating the healing journey. Each session builds on the previous as the client learns to see his or her heart through physical, mental, emotional, and spiritual lenses. The client's life experiences include biological, physiological, emotional, social, psychological, behavioral, and spiritual responses. An acknowledgement of an individual's uniqueness and how he or she experiences these events is gaining significant attention in the mental health field.

The healing journey is established with the overall goal of helping the client understand his or her life of problems, yet finding a true identity and acknowledgement of lessons learned from his or her life journey. Narrative reflection is the psychological approach to problem-solving, the foundational premise is that all people have a story to tell. The HeartPath practitioner works out of a psychospiritual foundation, focusing on assisting the client in formulating his or her story, which unfolds a unique and personal path. The path is the recognition of an individual's life experiences, together with, the synchronicity of the people in our lives and a God who loves us and guides us along our life path. A generated narrative allows the client to define who they are, based on his or her memories and perceptions of his or her life history and present life. This includes his or her roles in various social and personal settings. Relationships are a guideline and focus for the telling of a life story and need to be considered in order to produce healthy relationships.

The narrative approach is largely based in the post-modern ideas and psychological practices that reflect the practices of narrative therapy and provide people with new approaches to the predicaments presented in life. Narrative approaches utilized in healing work is gradually becoming recognized as one of the most influential and innovative processes of our time, as the cold reason and logic of the scientific age, makes way for the warmth and wisdom of the personal narrative. Therefore, looking at language within narrative processes, we see that the narrative not only affects how we frame our notions of the "self" and "identity," but also how practitioners deal with people searching for a sense of meaning of the world they live in. The mental themes that are generated from the telling of their story are powerful and possess healing qualities that are of value to the individual.

The HeartPath utilizes a combination of narrative techniques, guided imagery, meditation, prayer, and health consciousness, all as portals that lead to a life path as a meaning maker. When you allow a person to tell his or her story, there is a strong conviction that human beings are meaning makers. This is to propose that the client is active in the interpretation of experiences as he or she lives life day by day. Through lived experience, we strive to make sense of our world and our self, to find purpose and direction in the context of our own living—to find our HeartPath. Although many people tend to evaluate life on many different dimensions, meaning is often described in popular psychology as happy, satisfied, fully functional, self-actualized, fulfilled, well adjusted, mature, free of anxiety, liberated, enlightened, individuated, and saved.

Throughout history, mankind has been in search of his spirituality. It appears that our brains are somehow wired to ask questions such as, "Why am I here?" "Where do I come from?" And perhaps, "Where do I belong?" The HeartPath is a process that allows the client to tell his or her life story, so he or she can begin to connect meaning to those experiences both good and bad. The purpose of this process is to assist the client to see the connections that are taking place in his or her life story. This then begins to open spiritual eyes to a path for life that is specifically established for this journey called life. Life is a mystery and will remain a mystery, but has a way of giving us free will while gently leading us to our memory of God and our true selves. Seek God and listen for the heartbeat of intimacy that is beating within your inner heart and in the hearts of those around you.

> A new era, wrapped in the garment of approaching day, is dawning in the hearts of men; and soon again will the virgin Spirit of God shine forth from the heart and the door again will open, by which all who will may find entrance to a larger and fuller life. Young, vibrant, with perennial youth and hope and endeavor, the soul of man

> stands on the threshold of a new era, more glorious than any other that has brightened the sky since Creation's dawn. The Star of Bethlehem shone brighter at Jesus' birth than it had before but soon its brightness will be like a noonday sun, for this new light foretells the day when the Christ is born in the hearts of all men.
>
> —Excerpt from *Life and Teaching of the Masters of the Far East*, Vol. 2

According to the poem "To Him That Was Crucified," written by Walt Whitman, we are woven together by a common thread walking seemingly upheld and free. The common thread is within the inner spiritual sanctuary of our heart, and we believe the heart may be the seat of the Spirit.

My spirit to yours, dear brother,
Do not mind because many, sounding
your name, do not understand you;
I do not sound your name, but I understand you,
I specify you with joy O my comrade,
to salute you, and to salute
those who are with you, before and
since and those to come also;
That we all labor together, transmitting
the same charge and succession;
We few, equals, indifferent of
lands, indifferent of times;
We, enclosers of all continents, all
castes allowers of all theologies,
Compassionaters, perceivers, rapport of men;

We walk silent among disputes and
assertions, but reject not the
disputers, nor any thing that is asserted;
We hear the bawling and din we
are reach'd at by divisions,
jealousies, recriminations on every side;
They close peremptorily upon us,
to surround us, my comrade,
Yet we walk upheld, free, the whole
earth over, journeying up and
down, till we make our ineffaceable mark
upon time and the diverse eras;
Till we saturate time and eras, that
the men and women of races,
ages to come, may prove brethren
and lovers, as we are.

Throughout the book, we have placed forms of narrative from poetry, inspirational sayings, and scriptures. The HeartPath practitioner may choose to utilize this form of narrative processing within the sessions to create an atmosphere of inspiration and words of hope. Narratives read in a session should be presented by permission of the client, prior to sharing a reading, poem, or scripture. The practitioner should evaluate whether or not the reading will connect with a validation or summary of what has been shared in the session. For example, in the scripture below from 2 Corinthians, the client is reminded that in our troubled times, God is working in our inward self to strengthen us for eternal glory.

> For which cause we faint not; but though our outward man perish, yet the inward man is renewed day by day. For our light affliction, which is but for a moment, worketh for us a far more exceeding and eternal weight of glory; While we look not at the things which are seen, but for the things which are seen are temporal; but the things which are not seen are eternal.
>
> —2 Corinthians 4:16–18

The HeartPath practitioner takes into consideration everything that has an effect on the heart from the following perspectives:

1. Heart Physical Impact: including heart health from proper nutrition, heart health from movement, such as exercise, stretching, and breathing techniques, heart health from rest, such as sleep, and meditation.
2. Heart Mental Impact: including heart memory, heart-mind connection, and thoughts, feelings, and actions.
3. Heart Emotional Impact: including anger, worry, fear, hate, sadness, love, joy, and compassion.
4. Heart Spiritual Impact: including prayer, inner-heart sanctuary, unconditional love, and reconciliation.

Throughout history, the heart has symbolized the center or the core of our being. It is the synthesis not only of our affectivity, but also our freedom and consciousness, the place where we accept or reject the mystery of ourselves, human existence, and God. The heart, therefore, is a sacred space, an inner sanctuary for the Holy Spirit. It is here that we get in touch with the truth of our being and open our heart to the presence of God in our lives, our very "breath life."

Biblical writers regarded the heart as a symbol of the whole person. In the Old Testament, the word heart represents the principle of our personal life and the depth of our integration and insight. It is the center of our thinking, feeling, and deciding. This same view underlies the New Testament notion of the heart.

Augustinian spirituality looks at the "eyes of the heart," which become enlightened in faith and love of neighbor in order to see God. The desert writers of the fourth century wrote about "the prayer of the heart," which drove the desires of their search for God.

We want to focus on the statement "eyes of the heart" by sharing a poem written by Mattie J.T. Stepanek, from his book *Journey through Heartsongs*, which reflects the eyes of the heart as it points to the wind in our hearts. In the Bible, when reading verses of scripture that talk about the Spirit of God and our spirit, the Hebrew word *ruwach* is used in the Old Testament, which means mind, spirit, wind. In the New Testament, the Greek word translated spirit or Holy Spirit is *pneuma*, which in Greek means current of air (breath or breeze).

Meditation: The Wind in My Heart

This is not dream.
This is real.
I talk with God, and

Even if my eyes are closed,
I am awake, and I know.
Whichever direction
The wind is blowing,
I follow it.
And when the wind stops,
I stop where it stops,
And I see God.
Sometimes,
God looks like a golden harp
That is shaped like a silver flower.
We talk together about health, and
We talk about how babies
And other people die.
Then I hug and kiss God.
I can do that because
God is every-shape.
Every shape that the world has.
He is a circle, a triangle, every-shape.
He is even invisible.
And, he is even human.
So, we can hug God,
If we know how.
I understand, so I hug him.
God is everywhere the wind takes me.
The wind takes me to God, and
God takes the wind to me.
It asks me where I want to go
Without even saying anything, any word.
It just knows
It just knows.
I always see in the wind,
And so, I will follow the wind as it

Moves inside my world and
Inside my house and inside my heart.
I will trust the wind, and
I will let it take me wherever it is going,
Because God is in the wind.
God is the wind,
And I am here for God.
—Mattie J.T. Stepanek, August 1996

When we consider working with people with various issues, both relational and other pathologies (depression, anxiety, adjustment disorders), we begin to see the importance of healing the whole person. The HeartPath practitioner will assess all aspects of the heart-physical, heart-mind, heart-emotions, and heart-spiritual connection. The HeartPath is each individual's unique life path, and will continue to unfold before them as his or her life experiences, decisions, and meaning-making find a purpose and calling. The healing process is a phenomenon that takes place in the "telling of the story," and the understanding of the importance of seeing our heart as the center of our lives.

The Bible appears to reflect the heart of man as the central point within him where he is most himself. It is this point that God himself addresses. The *leb* or *lebab* of the Old Testament and the *kardia, koilia*, or *splancha* of the New Testament have the same meaning: true directive center of the person from which arises all his thoughts and feelings. The term heart, in its figurative sense as the center of being or consciousness, has a solid foundation in both the Old and New Testament of the Bible. The word heart, in its extended sense, is applied to both God and man. God truly intended the revelation of the heart of the Messiah. The revelation of the heart of the Savior belongs to the original message and meaning of sacred scripture. Although there is no specific mention of the veneration of the physical heart of Christ, this was later developed in mystical theology.

The Healing Power of the Telling of the Story

The HeartPath practitioner understands the healing power of the individual's telling of the story. The practitioner can facilitate throughout each healing session with the client the realization that there is significance in all of his or her life events. Having this understanding assists the client in making decisions for his or her future path and healing journey. The phenomenon of meaning making is a natural event in the told story of the client and whereupon the healing journey begins. The assumptions that people can develop strength and move on from adversity have been proven and supported from the personal testimonies of my own clientele. Practitioners also find it challenging in determining how the meaning-making process influences the outcome from these lived experiences, whether positive or negative.

As this book revealed, there has always been a HeartPath present within humans' lives. Consider Ecclesiastes in the Bible:

> The thing that hath been, it is that which shall be; and that which is done is that which shall be done: and there is no new thing under the sun. Is

there any thing whereof it may be said, "See, this is new?" it hath been already of old time, which was before us. There is no remembrance of things that are to come with those that shall come after."

Ecclesiastes 1:9–11

This book attempts to show a glimmer of how the heart has had significant meaning for many people throughout history. The heart is also one thing that we as humans all have in common. It is no respecter of person's color, size, cultural beliefs, or religion. The question proposed in this book is, how does a person become a HeartPath practitioner?

The single case study reflects the HeartPath approach to assist others find a healing journey. This case study reflects the complexity of a life story resulting in many losses of key people present in Mary's life. As Mary began to understand her core themes throughout her story, she began to reflect upon her sustaining faith in God throughout her life journey. It was easy for her to clearly see that it is important to give God the glory for teaching us through life lessons and never leaving nor forsaking us.

The HeartPath is significant in that it is a choice to have a pure heart before God. As HeartPath practitioners, we must lead by example. We also remain aware of the true healer—God. With an understanding of the science of compassion described earlier in the book, and the example that Jesus gave us, we may find the call to become a HeartPath practitioner. When we make a choice to be of service to others, more than likely, the HeartPath will play a part. The heart is the key to a lost mode of prayer.

The heart was also the first organ that God created when we were in our mother's womb. God does everything for a reason, and our focus over the years has seemingly moved away from the heart and focused more on the mind/ego and our material gains. When we begin to follow our heart, then we tap into the promise of God when he says he will give us the desires of our heart. What greater call is there than to be a vessel for God's healing for people who are seeking complete and whole healing? The Sacred Heart of Jesus says it all because his love for us is so strong that his heart is on fire for us. There is no greater love than this, no greater heart than his.

Appendix A
HeartPath Practitioner Guide and Checklist

HeartPath Evaluation

Discuss the four areas of our being: spirit, mind, emotion, and physical. (This can be measured with a simple scale of 1–10.)

Build a therapeutic corelationship, beginning with compassion for your client.

Ask client to begin by telling you his or her life story from as far back as he or she is comfortable sharing (varies by age of client).

Record and write the story and review the themes that arise from his or her story in a nonjudgmental reflection. Stories may also be in written form from the client. Drawings may also be incorporated.

HeartPath Interventions

Discuss with the client the core themes from his or her story.

Utilize guided imagery techniques to assist with the formulation of his or her life path, taking into consideration the unconscious material. Guided imagery should be focused on the image of his or her path and possible forks in the road.

Give the client an opportunity to rewrite his or her story from verbalized lived experiences.

Introduce the heart healing prayer based on the client's belief system as a portal to his or her soul.

Reinforce for the client that there is no separation between him or her, God's presence, and all of his creation.

Life Journey Process

Explain the importance of synchronicity and meaning-making of a client's lived experience.

Empower the client to acknowledge free will to make decisions and become cocreators in his or her life story, the ability to redefine his or her journey, and to reflect upon a heartfelt sense of life.

Reflect his or her life story, which reveals the presence of God, higher being, divine spirit, Creator. Reaffirm that we are never alone and walk always for all eternity in the presence of God.

Outcomes

Ability to manage anxiety and reduce fears in life.

Increased self-image reflective of God's energy and being.

Understanding of ongoing self-assessment of areas that need attending to—physical body, mind, emotions, and spiritual self, reflective of the telling of the story and validating one's life journey.

Understanding of the importance of daily spiritual practices that resonate with your soul by staying connected to the true and genuine self-sanctuary of the inner spiritual heart.

Glossary

Atrial Natriuretic Factor (ANF): ANF influences not only the blood vessels and kidneys, but also the mood-influencing adrenal glands and the brain.

Autobiographical Narrative: an opportunity for the client to reflect upon his or her own childhood, adolescent, and adult lived experiences in order to bring an understanding of important events in his or her life.

Cardio-energetics: teaches that God, or the Absolute, manifests as a divine, nonlocal, subtle energy that is everywhere and in everything. Cardio-energetics teaches that the heart can serve as a magnetic pole attracting that energy.

Electromagnetic Heart Functions: The heart has heart muscle cells that have the ability to contract spontaneously, and these cells work by generating electrical signals that spread to the rest of the heart and cause it to contract with a regular, steady beat.

Essence: the true being of a thing. Essence is what makes a thing what it is. The term essence derives from the Greek word *ousia*, which means the inner essential nature of a thing, the true being of a thing. The Latin *essentia*, from *esse,* means to be.

Explicit Memory: the conscious, intentional recollection of previous experiences and information.

Gnostics: Gnostic Christians believed that questioning one's faith is important. To know (gnosis) Christ was to seek a deeper and honest meaning for one's life. Gnosis led to wholeness in one's relationship to God and the world.

HeartPath Practitioner: a practitioner who offers counsel to his or her clients from a heart of compassion. This includes being fully present to the heart of God within the sacred space of the heart connection and a higher God consciousness. The HeartPath practitioner will see through a spiritual prism of compassion in order to help his or her clients connect to their own heart path, which is guided by the love and spiritual light within our being. The power of the told story/narrative approach reflects the healing journey. The HeartPath philosophy speaks to the balance of emotional, mental, spiritual, and physical self. It is a matter of the heart, and it is here that the true transformation for healing occurs.

Implicit Memory: a type of memory in which previous experiences aid in the performance of a task without conscious awareness of these previous experiences.

"L" energy: energy that travels at more than 186,000 miles per second and accounts for nonlocal effects of occurrences such

as remote healing and the power of intercessory prayer. The heart is uniquely composed of "L" energy, which it communicates and conveys in its own form, as well as piggybacked on the electromagnetic field (EMF) created by the heart.

Lived Experience: the lived human experience.

Narrative: Narrative has to do with addressing the stories by which people live life. These stories contain meaning for the individual, based on his or her interpretation of events and experiences. The meaning, in turn, influences him or her and can have significant effects and consequences for the person. Through retelling stories, one can find alternative ways of expressing his or her story. Robert and Holmes (1999) state that the narrative will develop accordingly by taking a different angle with a different thematic meaning, selecting events and experiences that are consistent with that theme.

Pedagogic Experience: Pedagogy requires a phenomenological sensitivity to lived experiences. The meaning of pedagogy can never be grasped in a single definition. Pedagogy also requires a hermeneutic ability to make interpretive sense of the phenomena of the life world in order to see the pedagogic significance of situations and relations. Pedagogy requires a way with language in order to allow the research process of textual reflection to contribute to one's pedagogic thoughtfulness and tact. The knowledge forms generated by a human science methodology are meant to serve the practical aims of pedagogy.

Phenomenological reduction: technical term that describes the phenomenological device that permits us to discover what Merleau-Ponty calls the spontaneous surge of the life world; to come to an understanding of the essential structure of something we need to reflect on it by practicing a certain reduction.

Phenomenology: the science of phenomena. According to Husserl, phenomenology became a descriptive method, as well as a human science movement, based on modes of reflection at the heart of philosophic and human science thought. Phenomenology must describe what is given to us in immediate experience without being obstructed by preconceptions and theoretical notions.

Psychocardiolgy: a new field emerging that goes back to the 1920s, relative to internal risk factors for heart disease. Psychological problems like depression, anxiety, and social isolation seem to predict both the development of disease in healthy patients and complications in those who are already patients, says Robert M. Carney, Ph.D., director of the Behavioral Medicine Center and a psychiatry professor at Washington University School of Medicine in St. Louis, Missouri.

Psychoneurocardiology: a new field that is a multifactorial intervention that includes diet, stress management, smoking cessation, exercise, and group support. Psychoneurocardiology is a developed lifestyle program involving changes in diet and stress management as an effective alternative to cardiac surgery and/or drugs.

Reconciliation: involves the reestablishment of a caring relationship in which mutually trustworthy behaviors and thoughts replace previously untrustworthy behaviors and attitudes.

Theme: the form of capturing the phenomenon one tries to understand: a) the need to make sense of the process of insightful invention, discovery, and disclosure; b) means to get at the notion or the phenomena being studied; and c) describes the content and a reduction of the notion.

References

Arterburn, Stephen (2005). *Healing is a Choice*. Nashville, Tennessee: Thomas Nelson, Inc.

Armour, J. and Ardell, J., Eds. (1994). *Neurocardiology*. New York, NY: Oxford University Press.

Bonaventure (d. 1274). *Itinerarium Mentis in Deum, Opera Omnia*, Vol. V, pp. 295–313.

Braden, Gregg (1998) *Beyond Zero Point*. (Audio tapes) New York, NY: Three Rivers.

Braden, Gregg (2000). *The Isaiah Effect*. New York, NY: Three Rivers Press.

Braden, Gregg (2008). *The Spontaneous Healing of Belief*. New York, NY: Hay House, Inc.

Capps, Annette (2007). *Quantum Faith*. England, Arkansas: Capps Publishing.

Childre, D. & Martin, H. (1999). *The HeartMath Solution*. New York, NY: HarperCollins Publishers, Inc.

Douglas-Klotz, Neil (1999). *The Hidden Gospel: Decoding the Spiritual Message of the Aramaic Jesus.* Wheaton, IL: Quest Books.

Egan, E. & Egan, K., O.S.B. Eds. (1992). *Blessed Are You: Mother Teresa and the Beatitudes.* New York, NY: MJF Books.

Einthoven, W. (1860–1927). *Nobel Lectures, Physiology or Medicine 1922–1941*, Elsevier Publishing Company, Amsterdam, 1965.

Epstein, D., Freeman, J., & Lobovits (1997). *Playful Approaches to Serious Problems: Narrative Therapy with Children and Their Families.* New York, NY: W.W. Norton & Company.

Epston, M. D. (1993). Internalizing discourses versus externalizing discourses. In S. Gilligan & R. Price (Eds.), *Therapeutic Conversations* (pp. 161–177). New York, NY: Norton. Retrieved from Capella Library, January 2008.

Fountain, Daniel E. (1999). *God, Medicine & Miracles: The Spiritual Factor in Healing.* Colorado Springs, Colorado: WaterBrook Press.

Fox, Matthew (1979). *A Spirituality Named Compassion: Uniting Mystical Awareness with Social Justice.* Rochester, Vermont: Inner Traditions International.

Freedman, J. & Combs, G. (1996). *Narrative Therapy: The Social Construction of Preferred Realities.* New York, NY Norton.

Heidegger, M. (1962). *Being and Time.* Macquarrie, J., and Robinson, E., (Eds.) New York, NY: Harper and Row.

Heidegger, M. (1971). *Poetry, Language, Thought.* New York, NY: Harper and Row.

Humphreys, C., & Thiara, R. (2003). Mental health and domestic violence: "I call it symptoms of abuse." *British Journal of Social Work*, 32, 209–226.

Husserl, E. (1900/1970). *The idea of phenomenology*. The Hague, Netherlands: Martinus Nijhoff.

Husserl, E. (1913/1982). *Ideas pertaining to pure phenomenology and to a phenomenological philosophy: General introduction to a pure phenomenology*. The Hague, Netherlands: Martinus Nijhoff.

Husserl, E. (1962/1977). *Phenomenological psychology*. (Trans. J. Scanlon). The Hague, Netherlands: Martinus Nijhoff.

Jung, C.G. (1963). Ed. Jaffe, A. *Memories, Dreams, Reflections*. New York: NY: Vintage Books,.

Klein, P. & Westcott, M. R. (1994). "The changing character of phenomenological psychology." *Canadian Psychology*, 35, 133–158. Retrieved from Capella Library, March 2008.

Lamsa, George (1933). *Holy Bible: From the Ancient Eastern Text from the Aramaic of the Peshitta*. New York, NY: A. J. Holman Company.

Licensed Spiritual Health Coach Philosophy/License Information, Retrieved from www.spiritualhealth-coach.com, June, 2008.

Lucado, Max (2002). *A Love Worth Giving: Living in the Overflow of God's Love.* Nashville, Tennessee: W. Publishing Group a Division of Thomas Nelson, Inc.

MacDonald, Gordon (1984) *Restoring Joy.* Edison, NJ: Inspirational Press.

McAdams, D. P. & Josselson, R. (1995). "Narrative and psychological understanding." *Journal of Personality and Social Psychology*, 58, 330–343.

McFeature, B. J. (2009). *Exploring the Lived Experience of Adult Women Victimized by Partner Abuse.* Kolin, Germany: LAP Lambert Academic Publishing AG & Co. KG.

Meichenbaum, D. (1988). "What happens when the brute data of psychological inquiry are meanings: Nurturing a dialogue between hermeneutics and empiricism." *Hermeneutics and Psychological Theory.* Messer, S., Sass, L., and Woolfolk, R., (Eds.) Rutgers University Press, New Brunswick, NJ.

Merleau-Ponty, M. (1962). *Phenomenology of Perception.* (Smith, C., Trans.) Atlantic City, NJ: Humanities Press.

Moriarty, Michael (1993). "The Buddhist Sanskrit text with interlinear vocabulary." *Sociology Religion Eastern Journal*, Berkeley, CA: DharmaNet.

Morgan, Alice (2000). *What is Narrative Therapy?* New York, NY: Gecko Publishers.

Mullino-Moore, Mary Elizabeth (1998). *Teaching from the Heart: Theology and Educational Method.* Philadelphia, PA: Trinity Press International.

National Geographic In the Womb DVD (2005). Viewed in January 2007 as seen on the National Geographic Channel.

National Institutes of Health. The Seventh Report of the Joint National Committee on Prevention, Detection, Evaluation, and Treatment of High Blood Pressure. NIH Publication. 2003. No. 03–5233.

New King James Version of the Bible. Copyright Thomas Nelson.

O'Donnell, T. (1989). *Heart of the Redeemer.* Manassas, VA: Trinity Communications.

Ornish, Dean (1993) "Opening your heart: Physically, emotionally, spiritually." *Noetic Sciences Review* 28, Winter 1993 (page 304).

Pearsall, Paul (1998). *The Heart's Code.* New York, NY: Broadway Books.

Roberts, G. & Holmes, J. (Eds.). (1999). *Healing Stories: Narrative in Psychiatry and Psychotherapy.* Oxford, NY: Oxford University Press.

Shapiro. F. (1999). "Eye movement desensitization and reprocessing (EMDR) and the anxiety disorders: Clinical research implications of an integrated psychotherapy treatment." *Journal of Anxiety Disorders*, 13, 35–67.

Siegel, D. J. (1999). *The Developing Mind. How Relationships and the Brain Interact to Shape Who We Are.* New York, NY: Guilford Press.

Spalding, B. T. (1927). *Life and Teaching of the Masters of the Far East, Vol. 2.* Camarillo, CA: DeVorss Publications.

Sphar, A. and Smith, Argile (2001). *Helping Hurting People: A Handbook on Reconciliation-focused Counseling and Preaching*. Self-Published–USA.

Strong, Mary (1948). *Letters of the Scattered Brotherhood.* New York, NY: HarperCollins Publishers.

Tart, Charles T. (1975). *Transpersonal Psychologies: Perspectives on the Mind From Seven Great Spiritual Traditions.* New York, NY: Harper & Row Publishers, Inc.

Tauler, John (1556). *Exercitia D. Joannis Thauleri,* tr. Nicolao Eschio (Lugduni: S.B. Honorati) (pp. 411–412; cf. Richstaetter, opl. Cit., p. 127).

Van Manen, M. (1990). *Researching Lived Experience: Human Science for an Action Sensitive Pedagogy.* Ontario, Canada: The University of Western Ontario.

WebMD Medical Reference Provided in Collaboration with the Cleveland Clinic. Retrieved on April 13,

2008 from http://www.webmd.com/fitness-exercise/exercise-healthy-heart.

White, Michael (1995) *Re-authoring lives: Interviews and Essays*. Adelaide: Dulwich Centre Publications.

Wolpe, Rabbi David (1999). *Making Loss Matter: Creating Meaning in Difficult Times*. New York, NY: Riverhead Books, The Berkley Publishing Company.

Notes

e|LIVE

listen|imagine|view|experience

AUDIO BOOK DOWNLOAD INCLUDED WITH THIS BOOK!

In your hands you hold a complete digital entertainment package. Besides purchasing the paper version of this book, this book includes a free download of the audio version of this book. Simply use the code listed below when visiting our website. Once downloaded to your computer, you can listen to the book through your computer's speakers, burn it to an audio CD or save the file to your portable music device (such as Apple's popular iPod) and listen on the go!

How to get your free audio book digital download:

1. Visit www.tatepublishing.com and click on the e|LIVE logo on the home page.
2. Enter the following coupon code: 5cbf-7d8b-aa0e-6c79-e11d-bf64-82e0-b4cb
3. Download the audio book from your e|LIVE digital locker and begin enjoying your new digital entertainment package today!